CRUSH YOUR GOALS!

"Goals aren't about being perfect; they're about being better than you were before."

CRUSH YOUR GOALS!

Trade Your Old, Tired Resolutions for an Exciting Goal Setting Strategy that Gets Results!

AUSTIN BOLLINGER

Founder of DailyNewYears.com

Got Your Workbook?

Grab a copy today!

Crush Your Goals! wasn't written to be read cover-to-cover in one sitting; it was designed to be read with strategic breaks in between every chapter. The **Crush Your Goals! Workbook** was developed to help maximize your performance by walking you through the lessons and techniques found within each chapter.

I encourage you to grab your copy of the workbook before diving into the first chapter. Trust me; you'll be glad you did.

- ⊘ Download the PDF version of the workbook for free at www.crushyourgoalsbook.com/resources.

- ⊘ Or, buy a physical copy of the workbook on Amazon and keep both copies together on your bookshelf.

Copyright © 2020 B&B Media, L.L.C.

Published in the United States by Daily New Year's, a division of B&B Media, L.L.C., Missouri.

All rights reserved.

No part of this publication may be reproduced, distributed, or transmitted in any form or by any means, including photocopying, recording, or other electronic or mechanical methods, without the prior written permission of the publisher, except in the case of brief quotations embodied in critical reviews and certain other noncommercial uses permitted by copyright law.

Although the author and publisher have made every effort to ensure that the information in this book was correct at press time, the author and publisher do not assume and hereby disclaim any liability to any party for any loss, damage, or disruption caused by errors or omissions, whether such errors or omissions result from negligence, accident, or any other cause.

Adherence to all applicable laws and regulations, including international, federal, state, and local governing professional licensing, business practices, advertising, and all other aspects of doing business in the US, Canada, or any other jurisdiction is the sole responsibility of the reader and consumer.

Neither the author nor the publisher assumes any responsibility or liability whatsoever on behalf of the consumer or reader of this material. Any perceived slight of any individual or organization is purely unintentional.

The resources in this book are provided for informational purposes only and should not be used to replace the specialized training and professional judgment of a health care or mental health care professional.

Neither the author nor the publisher can be held responsible for the use of the information provided within this book. Please always consult a trained professional before making any decision regarding treatment of yourself or others.

ISBN 978-1-7345507-3-3 (Hardback)
ISBN 978-1-7345507-0-2 (Paperback)
ISBN 978-1-7345507-1-9 (Ebook)
ISBN 978-1-7345507-2-6 (Workbook)

Categories: 1. Personal Success 2. Personal Transformation 3. Success

Printed in the United States of America

Cover Design by Austin Bollinger

First Edition

Dedicated to my loving wife and lifelong best friend, Callie, who I love more than everything.

Contents

Prologue 13
Introduction 5
Getting Started with This Book 11

Section 1: Cultivating a Goal Getter's Mindset 17

1. Find and Embrace Your Why 19
2. Overcome the Six Fears of Goal Setting 33
3. How to Build Rock-Solid Self-Confidence 55
4. Develop a Goal Getter's Mindset 71

Section 2: Getting Started with Goal Setting 105

5. The FOCUSED Framework 107
6. Four Types of Goals to Start Setting Today 121
7. Prioritize Like a Pro & Crush Your Goals in Record Time 143
8. The Best Tools for Tracking Your Goals 171

Section 3: Establishing a System for Success 191

9. Assemble a Support Team 193

10. The Four Cs of High-Performance Goal Setting........................211

11. Develop a Daily, Success-Driven Routine 229

12. Build Momentum Using the Domino Effect.............................247

Section 4: Dealing with Difficulties 263

13. How to Stay Motivated...265

14. Five Tips for Overcoming Obstacles 275

15. Moving Beyond Failure..289

16. Take Action Today!..301

Epilogue 309

Acknowledgments..313

Prologue

"Outstanding people have one thing in common: an absolute sense of mission."

– Zig Ziglar

Hi, my name is Austin Bollinger, and my mission is to help you ditch your New Year's resolutions, and instead help you crush your goals every single day, and all year long.

I'm a husband to my high school sweetheart, Callie. I'm a doggy dad, proud uncle (five nephews and one niece), weightlifter, beer lover, lifetime learner, and I'm a Goal Getter. I love spending time with my wife, my family, and of course, my pups. I'm obsessed with goal setting, but as you'll see in a minute, it wasn't always that way.

Currently, I'm the Chief Operations Officer for a Digital Agency in Cape Girardeau, Missouri, called Element 74. I went to college for a degree in graphic design but fell in love with video production soon after.

From there, I cycled my way through various skills, jobs, passions, and so on. For as long as I can remember, I've always been an ambitious, driven, and self-motivated person, but for most of my life, I struggled with clarity and focus in where I wanted to go.

For a long time, I didn't have clear, long-term goals for my life. I'm not even sure I ever practiced goal setting regularly. Sure, every year I would set a New Year's resolution, and I might have a random fitness goal in mind for the year, but nothing ever too meaningful or future focused.

Sometime in 2014, I got tired of postponing my self-improvement and my future. I got tired of waiting to set one huge goal on January first, only to quit less than forty-five days later. I was frustrated, but sometime that year, something finally clicked!

I began writing some goals down, started consuming personal development content, and I was building a routine around my goals. Instead of waiting for January first, I decided to start setting daily and weekly goals for myself.

Back then, most of my goals revolved around fitness, and at the time I was training for the 1,000-pound club at my local gym. [1] Now, this goal took a long time to train for, and I later increased the goal to 1,250 pounds, so I'll skip ahead a couple of years.

One fall morning in October 2017, I was following my usual routine: wake up at 4:45, head off to the gym, tune into a podcast, and hit the weights before work. As I was listening to a podcast, resting for another lift, a thought hit me like a bolt of lightning! What if more people set goals every month,

---

[1] The 1,000-pound club is a weight lifting accomplishment where a weight lifter combines their one-rep maximum for the Deadlift, Squat, and Bench Press for a cumulative total. The total should be equal to or greater than 1,000 pounds. Many gyms have clubs for 1,000, 1,250, and 1,500 pounds.

Prologue

every week, and every day? What if we could harness the energy and motivation of New Year's Day every day?

No sooner than the idea jumped into my head, a name and mission followed: Daily New Year's, a blog about starting new things and striving for continual improvement all year long. I raced home and wrote it down in my journal. My blog, DailyNewYears.com, was born!

Since that fall day in 2017, I have been pursuing my goals with passionate energy. I've been pouring everything I have into Daily New Year's.

I'm not perfect—not even close! I love talking about goal setting, personal development, and high performance, but I make mistakes and sometimes I struggle to take my own advice, but I'm working to become Better Every Day. [2]

My Daily New Year's journey is what inspired this book. I wanted to invite people all over the world to join me in working to become Better Every Day through the power of daily goal setting.

We can all see our dreams come true by taking action towards our goals and building massive momentum in our lives.

I hope you're ready, because if I've done my job well, this book is about to change your life.

If you're frustrated with how you've fared with resolutions or goal setting in the past, don't worry. This book is different, and if you stick with me until the end, you're going to learn how to ditch your resolutions and instead start seeing the success you've been looking for.

So if you're ready, let's dive in and start crushing our goals.

---

[2] *Better Every Day* is a theme, a mantra, if you will, and you're going to see it throughout this book because it's something I try to live by.

Introduction

"The secret to getting ahead is getting started."
— Mark Twain

Are you the kind of person who wants to achieve massive success in your life and finally see your dreams come true?

Are you still looking for the best way to do that? If so, I feel your pain because I've been there.

You've scoured the internet, searched the bookstores high and low, watched countless videos on YouTube, all while trying to find answers to the questions that have evaded you for years.

You know the questions—they're the questions you think about all the time:

- ⊘ "Why can't I earn more money?"

- ✓ "Why can't I lose weight?"
- ✓ "Why can't I quit smoking?"
- ✓ "Why aren't I more motivated?"
- ✓ "Why can't I achieve my goals?"

Whatever your questions are, you've likely done everything you can, but there's still something holding you back, but what is it?

People just like us have been asking these questions for years.

Fortunately, I discovered the answer for myself in October 2017.

I noticed that every year, countless people—people just like you and me—give up on their goals and dreams because they set the bar too high with their resolutions on New Year's Eve.

The "New Year, New You" mantra starts appearing everywhere around mid-December, giving us all a huge surge of motivation. But the motivation doesn't last, and neither do our resolutions.

New Year's resolutions DO NOT work. They've been holding us back for decades and here's why:

- ⊗ The very nature of setting a resolution on New Year's Eve promotes procrastination. When we wait for New Year's Day to set our biggest goals, we put off what we could start today.
- ⊗ Setting one huge goal at the beginning of each year makes it nearly impossible to stay focused on that goal all year long. Who could blame us? A year is a long time to stay focused on one huge thing.
- ⊗ Because of this procrastination and lack of focus,

Introduction

most of us tend to set the wrong goals, such as trying to lose a "quick" 45 pounds instead of practicing proper diet and exercise all year long. This cycle leads to discouragement and the desire to quit.

The good news is there's a better way!

Since October of 2017, I've been working to build a community who works toward achieving massive success in their lives every day.

We don't rely on New Year's resolutions to get started—we don't wait for next month, next week, or even tomorrow. We take action towards our dreams every single day.

We understand that progress is better than perfection, and that postponing our dreams will only hold us back in the long run. We're tired of starting, stopping, and failing—we're better than that.

We work towards our goals with unstoppable momentum so that we can become Better Every Day.

We are Goal Getters, and we're only one goal away from achieving GREATNESS in our lives!

Does that sound like something you want to be a part of?

Are you ready to ditch your resolutions and focus on becoming Better Every Day?

If you're pumped up and ready to learn how to crush your biggest goals but are feeling a little bit overwhelmed, take a deep breath and relax. I'm with you all the way.

In the following pages, you're going to learn a new goal-setting framework, several different types of goals and goal-setting strategies, tips, and tricks for staying motivated and overcoming obstacles, and so much more.

This book was written to be a guide that will actively lead you forward into the world of successful goal setting. Every chapter includes information on exciting and effective strategies to help you see the success you've been searching for. The accompanying workbook also includes exercises and guided assessments to get you started quicker and help you stay on the right track.

If there's one thing I know for sure, it's that action and momentum are the keys to success in any endeavor. Buying this book was your first action towards making your dreams come true—working through its pages will begin to build your momentum.

Together, we're about to learn a new goal-setting strategy that will make achieving success in your life as simple as possible. All you have to do is keep reading.

Thanks for joining me. I'm so glad you're here.

Austin Bollinger
Founder of Daily New Years

Introduction

Getting Started with This Book

"You don't have to be good to start ... you just have to start to be good!"

– Joe Sabah

The following book is a compilation of various teachings, strategies, methods, notes, advice, and action plans that I've been using to better my own life for the past couple of years. I've assembled them into this book so that they might help you do the same in your own life.

This book has four sections.

The first section, "Cultivating a Goal Getter's Mindset," will help you understand the mentality of someone seeking to become Better Every Day. It will also help you identify your *why*, overcome your fears around goal setting, and teach you how to build confidence around your goals.

The second section, "Getting Started with Goal Setting," will teach you a brand new goal-setting framework, different types of goals you can use, and how to prioritize and track your goals.

The third section, "Developing a System of Success," will show you how to build a network of people who will help you succeed, and it will teach you how to use habits, routines, and momentum to build upon your success day after day.

The fourth and final section, "Dealing with Difficulties," will guide you through the challenges of goal setting. The chapters in this section will teach you how to stay motivated, overcome obstacles and setbacks, how to move beyond failures when they arise, and how to take action towards your dreams.

As you'll soon discover, each chapter was designed to help you in a specific way. Some teach new strategies that will help you crush your goals while others were designed to help strengthen your new Goal Getter's mindset. While each chapter is unique, each one contains a recap at the end to help compress the chapter into a few key takeaways.

Chapter Recaps

Each chapter covers a great deal of content, so the recaps were designed to provide you with a snapshot from the chapter. These include key takeaways, core ideas and principles, definitions, memorable quotes, exercises, and more.

After completing this book, you may wish to refer back to its lessons from time to time. As you continue to use this book in the years to come, revisit the chapter recaps for a refresher on the contents of each chapter.

If the recap doesn't include the content that you feel was most important or relevant to you, use the accompanying

Getting Started

workbook to jot down your own notes along the way and complete the exercises and self-assessments that have been designed to help drive each lesson home.

The Crush Your Goals! Workbook

This book is going to cover a great deal of information, strategies, hands-on exercises, self-assessments, guided reflections, and so much more. **I do not recommend reading this book cover to cover without taking time to complete each chapter's materials as you go along.** Not doing so will be like drinking from a fire hydrant and the information overload is likely to overwhelm you.

The *Crush Your Goals! Workbook* was designed to help you process and apply the lessons learned throughout the book at a steady and comfortable pace.

You can download, save, and print the workbook **for free** at www.crushyourgoalsbook.com. However, I recommend purchasing the matching workbook for a small, additional fee. This will allow you to keep the main book and the workbook together on your bookshelf, making referencing your notes and assessments as easy as possible in the future.

The workbook follows the same structure and table of contents as the main book, making it easy to follow along as you read the book or for cross-referencing at a later time. Each chapter in the workbook contains space for taking notes and jotting down your ideas as well as several worksheets or assessments.

Chapter Notes

The chapter notes pages in the workbook were designed to give you space to capture your thoughts, feelings, and key takeaways.

Most books don't provide an area for notes, and if they do, it's either a small space at the end of the chapter or it's lost somewhere in the back of the book. This leaves the reader to flip back and forth as they need to jot down their ideas. I've been there and done that and it's frustrating.

Alternatively, I've tried taking notes in various notebooks, but referring back to these thoughts and ideas is often a daunting task. "Which journal had my notes for this book again? Was it the black moleskin I was using last year or was it my 2019, Q2 planner?" What a mess!

Many of the books I own contain crammed, hard-to-read notes in the margins of the pages because, oftentimes, that's the only place I can find to make notes that I'm guaranteed to find later. However, that still requires a great deal of flipping through pages and searching for particular notes and ideas.

This is why I highly recommend either buying the accompanying *Crush Your Goals! Workbook* or downloading the free version at www.crushyourgoalsbook.com. In my opinion, the official workbook is the perfect way to keep your notes right next to the book on your bookshelf.

This book was designed to help you maximize your growth. As you read, new thoughts and ideas will undoubtedly come to you. When this happens, flip to the chapter notes pages in the workbook and record your thoughts before they escape you. You never know how important an idea may be later, so be sure to write them down as they occur to you.

I recommend taking notes in the workbook versus jotting them down in a separate notebook that may get lost later on. Doing so will help make the book even more valuable to you as you refer back to it in the future.

Chapter Worksheets

Finally, each chapter includes at least one worksheet, self-assessment, or guided reflection. Some may even contain a series of useful worksheets to help guide you through the material.

As you'll see in the coming chapters, all the learning in the world will do you no good if you don't take action on what you're learning.

The chapter worksheets have been designed to help you take action immediately upon completing the chapter and while the content is fresh in your mind. Please don't skip these exercises. The lessons in the book build upon one another, so skipping any one of them may leave you scratching your head later.

Upon completing a chapter, finish jotting down all of your organic thoughts and feelings in the chapter notes and then proceed on to these worksheets. As you do, please keep in mind that, like with all self-assessments, **100 percent truth and honesty with yourself is vital for personal development.**

We cannot grow if we do not acknowledge our weaknesses, past failures, self-limiting beliefs, and so on. As you complete the worksheets, be as honest with yourself as you can be. It will be worth it in the end; I promise!

Without further ado, let's dive into the first chapter and get started in developing our Goal Getter's mindset.

SECTION 1

CULTIVATING A GOAL GETTER'S MINDSET

Find and Embrace Your Why

"If you get a big enough 'why' you can do anything."
– Tony Robbins

Goal setting is one of my biggest passions. Sounds kind of odd, right? I love a lot of normal things, too: my wife, my dogs, Marvel movies, and drinking a good cold beer on a beach somewhere, but I also love goal setting. Some people have a passion for philanthropy, the environment, politics, or any number or combination of things.

Me? I'm passionate about setting goals, talking about goals, and helping other people crush their goals.

I think a lot of people find my passion for goals a little unusual or maybe even peculiar. Others find it "crazy," especially when they find out that I get up at four in the morning to make time for all of my goals. This book, the gym, my blog—it all takes time, and because I'm mildly obsessed with crushing my goals, I make the time. But as you'll see throughout this chapter and this entire book, how I achieve my goals (four a.m. mornings included) is not nearly as important as *why* I want to achieve the goals I'm pursuing.

Some people can't understand my love for goal setting because, frankly, they've tried and failed in the past. I totally get it! I've done the same thing over and over again throughout my life.

Maybe that's why you bought this book. Perhaps you've tried setting goals in the past and didn't see the success that you wanted or you failed altogether. Perhaps you picked it up because the cover openly bashes New Year's resolutions and you were intrigued because resolutions have let you down over and over, and year after year. Or maybe you grabbed this book because you've never tried setting goals and you didn't know where to start.

Regardless of why you bought my book, I want to ask you a very important question before we go too much further: *why* are you really reading this book?

What do you want your life to be like? What is it you hope to achieve? What are your biggest and wildest dreams? Take a second to get a clear picture of those things in your mind.

Assuming that several things start swirling around in your brain, you might be wondering *how* you're going to go about achieving your goals or making your dreams come true. You might start thinking about getting up at four a.m. yourself just to have enough time to get it all done. That's where a lot people get overwhelmed and give up before they even start, but I want to shift your focus away from the *how* and onto the *why*. The how will come. Trust me; there are fifteen more chapters about the how.

First, let's talk about the *why* behind our goals.

Discover and Embrace Your Why

Starting with "Why"

One of my favorite speakers and authors Tony Robbins teaches that "If you get a big enough *why* you can do anything." [1]

This idea is one of the most impactful things I've ever heard, and he's not the only one teaching this concept. Simon Sinek has been spreading this message in his 2009 New York Times Best Selling book, *Start with Why*.

I won't restate all of Simon's concepts and ideas in this book [1], but in short, he says that "Your 'why' is the purpose, cause or belief that inspires you." [2]

The problem is that so many people start with *what* they want to do and then skip straight to the *how*. For example:

> "I want to lose weight, so I need to limit my caloric intake and start exercising more often." [2]

With that example, we have the *what* and *how*, but we don't have a *why*. If knowing how to lose weight were the answer to having that year-round beach bod that everyone seems to want, more people would. But knowing *how* is not enough.

Instead, you have to ask, "Why do I want to lose weight?" Before you jump to the *how*, you have to start with *why*.

This is something that so many people overlook, but taking the time to connect with your *why* will lead to high levels of intrinsic motivation, which we'll look at more in chapter 13.

---

1 If you want to know more, you can check out Simon's story and buy his book at www.startwithwhy.com.

2 As a note, I'll be using weight loss as an example several times throughout this book, not because I think we all need to shed a few extra pounds, but because I believe it's all a goal to which most of us can relate.

With a new understanding of the importance of *why*, I've looked back throughout my life and have had several "aha" moments—moments where having a strong *why* was so glaringly obvious and I want to share one of those moments with you here.

I started calling my grandma "Ninnie" before I could really talk. I'm not sure why. Maybe my family members were trying to get me to say "Nanna" and the word just didn't come out right. Or maybe it was just one of those cute things kids say when they can't fully talk yet. Either way, the name stuck, so that's how I will refer to her in this story.

Growing up I remember Ninnie smoking. She smoked in the house, in the car, and pretty much anywhere else. Like a lot of people from her generation, Ninnie grew up smoking and the habit had her locked in for well over forty years.

I remember her trying to quit several different times throughout my childhood and early teenage years, but she always had a difficult time with it.

Can you imagine smoking for that long and trying to quit? I sure as heck can't!

However, in 2002, my cousin Jacob was born. Jacob was Ninnie's first grandchild since my sister and me, ten or eleven years prior.

Suddenly, there was a newborn baby in the house and it wasn't the sixties or seventies anymore. New, concrete information was out: smoking causes cancer and secondhand smoke was unhealthy for bystanders. It was no longer a theory and Ninnie knew it, or so I assume. She never quite said as much, but in 2002, I'm proud to say that Ninnie finally kicked the habit.

Sadly, she's no longer with us, so I can't ask her what changed, but I believe that she thought she had seen all her grandkids grow up to be adults, but her youngest son, my uncle, suddenly gave her a whole new generation of grandchildren to love and watch grow up. She wanted a safe, smoke-free house for her grandchildren, and she wanted to improve her health so that she may live longer.

It wasn't obvious to me earlier in my life, but clearly she found her *why*!

Even after trying several times before and failing, she quit smoking in a very short amount of time after connecting with her new *why*. I don't know about you, but I think that's powerful and inspiring.

My Ninnie stumbled upon her why nearly by accident when my aunt and uncle announced their pregnancy, but we need to be more proactive about finding our own whys.

Let's take a look at how to do just that.

How to Find Your Why

Simon Sinek has an overarching why for his whole life:

> "My why is to inspire people to do what inspires them so that, together, we can change our world for the better." [3]

However, if you want to start smaller, you can set a *why* for your individual goals or different areas in your life.

Remember my goal to get into the 1,000-pound club in 2015 and then the 1,250-pound club the year after?

Why on Earth did I set that goal?

Well, I wanted to prove to myself that I could do it—that was my *why*! Prior to having this goal, I would miss the gym frequently or just go through the motions with minimal effort. But with my *why* I had focus!

Soon after setting this goal and connecting with my *why*, I found that making good decisions in other areas of my life became easier, too.

I started eating better, getting more sleep, drinking less alcohol, and I never missed a workout Monday through Friday, all because I knew those things would help me achieve my goal.

But maybe most people would consider my *why* for that goal to be a weak *why*. When I started my blog, Daily New Year's in 2017, I wanted to help people overcome the New Year's resolution trap by helping them to start setting goals year round? Why?

I had fallen into that same trap myself for years, postponing my self-improvement for ten months at a time only to set another failed resolution the year after. I was sick of wasting time, and I was positive that other people were, too. I looked around and saw countless people doing the same thing, and I wanted to make a powerful impact on the world around me. That was my *why* behind the blog.

I see my blog, and now this book, as a platform for positive change. Setting New Year's resolutions is a fun tradition, but it's no way to go about improving our lives. I want to get as many people setting goals as possible because I believe we can all achieve the lives we've been dreaming of, we just have to set goals and take it day by day.

Thinking about helping people, my *why*, is what fills me with a passionate drive towards my goal of blogging, podcasting, and building a community. Perhaps that's a stronger, better *why* than the *why* I had for my weightlifting goals.

Discover and Embrace Your Why

The point is, if what you really want to do is worth doing, then you should be able to find a *why* that excites you.

To get started ask yourself *why* you want to do something. Then for every answer you come up with, ask *why* for that, too. Keep going until you find the most meaningful answer. It may take some vulnerability and honesty, and it may get a little annoying, but you'll know the answer when you get to it.

Here's an example:

- ⊗ "I want to run a half-marathon." ... Why?
- ⊗ "Because I need exercise." ... Why?
- ⊗ "Because I don't like the way I feel." ... Why?
- ⊗ "Because I'm overweight and I want to lose 30 pounds." ... Why?
- ✓ "Because being overweight makes me feel tired, sluggish, and self-conscious about the way I look. I want to feel better about myself. I want to feel good about how I look."

Bingo!

Now your *why* for running a half-marathon isn't an empty goal—it's a goal with a significant meaning behind it. You're NOT running to just to be running, you're NOT running to lose weight—you're running to feel better about yourself and that's huge!

Maybe you want to run a half-marathon but your *why* is totally different. That's okay! It should be. I'm training for one right now, and I'm doing it to improve my cardiovascular health. But just like the 1,250-pound club, I also want to see if I can do it. Maybe that's your *why*, too. Whatever it is, make your *why* something that excites and inspires you.

It may be difficult, but keep asking yourself *why* until you find an answer that resonates with you and excites you. That's what's going to keep you going. However, *why* provides more than energy and motivation; it also provides clarity.

Why Provides Clarity

I'm always looking for the *why* in everything I do because it helps me find my motivation, but it also helps me say no when I need to.

We all encounter endless opportunities in life, from going out with friends on Friday night to accepting new job offers. Opportunities are everywhere!

A couple of years ago I was asked to join not one but two boards of directors. Thinking this would be prestigious, I accepted both without thinking about *why* I should join either.

It wasn't long after I joined both that I began dreading the meetings. I didn't want to go, and I didn't really know why! They had fantastic missions and were doing good work in the community. I felt awful for not wanting to be more involved, but it's the way I felt.

It took some reflection, but I discovered where my internal struggle was coming from. At the time, I had just started my blog and would have rather spent all of my free time working on producing valuable content than be sitting in board meetings. Serving on these boards was consuming more time than I was ready to give, but I didn't want to quit on these two organizations either.

After wrestling with the decision for a long time, I finally realized that my heart was not in these two organizations. The reason I had joined—my *why*—was extremely weak. I thought that being on a board of directors was something I needed to do, but it wasn't something I wanted to do.

After finding that sense of clarity, I decided to quit both boards and instead focus on building a community around Daily New Year's. As much as I hated to resign, a major weight had been lifted.

Now I realize that saying yes to something almost always means having to say no to something else.

It's Okay to Say "No"

We only have so much time to do the things we want, so it's critical that we focus on the things we want to do—the things we're deeply connected and engaged with.

I learned that what we say no to is probably more important than what we say yes to. Have you ever heard the saying, "Every yes must be defended by a thousand no's?" It's true!

When we say yes to one thing, we have to say no to countless other things to protect our time. Otherwise saying yes to too many things could mean that you don't get anything done.

To keep this from happening, we have to evaluate every opportunity. When you're faced with a new opportunity and you're leaning towards saying yes but you're unsure, ask yourself these questions first:

- ⊗ Do you feel obligated to say yes?
- ⊗ Are you afraid of confrontation, so you only want to say yes to avoid saying no?
- ⊗ Do you want to say no, but you don't want to let the person asking down?
- ⊗ Do you genuinely want to say yes? Will you still be excited about this opportunity a week from now?

Saying yes for the wrong reasons will leave you with a situation that you won't be happy with, and it could cause you to have to say no to something you want more later on.

So if you can't find a good reason to say yes—a *why*— then just say no.

It's okay to say no, especially if your heart isn't in it.

What's Your Why?

As you move deeper into this book, you're going to be learning more concepts and strategies for successful goal setting, but it all starts with *why*.

Learning how to set goals, what kind of mindset will serve you best, how to form an accountability group—none of what you're going to learn will matter if you don't first connect with your *why*.

Your *why* is what will keep you going when you're tired or when you just don't feel like it. Your *why*, as you'll see in a later chapter, is what powers your motivation, keeping you charged for the amazing lifetime of goal setting that lies ahead.

Your *why* is one of the most important factors to your goal-setting success—the foundation, so to speak. Before we dive into the next chapter and learn how to overcome the six fears of goal setting, use the following pages to reflect on your goals and identify a *why* for each of them.

Discover and Embrace Your Why

CHAPTER RECAP

Key Takeaways

- ✓ The problem that so many people experience with goal setting is starting with **what** they want to do and then skipping straight to the **how** without ever considering their *why*.

- ✓ Taking time to identify a strong *why* will lead to high levels of **Intrinsic Motivation** and improved levels of success over the long term.

- ✓ **Finding your *why*** is as easy as asking yourself "why?" over and over again until you reach a deep, emotional reason for your goal. When you find it, you'll feel it.

    For example:
    — "I want to run a half-marathon."
        Why?
    — "Because I need exercise."
        Why?
    — "Because I'm overweight and I want to lose thirty pounds."
        Why?
    — "Because I don't like the way I feel."
        Why?
    — "Because being overweight makes me feel tired, sluggish, and self-conscious about the way I look. I want to feel better about myself. I want to feel good about how I look."

- ✓ ***Why* provides clarity.** Not all things are worth doing. If you can't find a meaningful *why* for something, perhaps it's not a something you really want to do.

Discover and Embrace Your Why

- ✓ **It's okay to say "no"** to opportunities that don't excite you or support your goals. Saying yes to things you don't truly want to do subtracts time and energy from the things you do want to do.
- ✓ **Time and energy are limited resources**, both of which you should protect and use wisely.
- ✓ **Finding your *why* is the foundation for your goals.** The goal setting strategies found throughout this book will not matter if you don't first discover and embrace the *why* behind each your goals.

Memorable Quotes

☆ *"If you get a big enough why you can do anything."* —Tony Robbins

☆ *"Your why is the purpose, cause or belief that inspires you."* —Simon Sinek

☆ *"Every Yes must be defended by a thousand No's."* —Jeff Walker.

Put it into Practice

▶ Use the corresponding worksheets to examine your current goals and ask: *"Why do I want to achieve these goals?"*

▶ Consider postponing or abandoning any goals that have weak *whys*.

Overcome the Six Fears of Goal Setting

"Inaction breeds doubt and fear. Action breeds confidence and courage. If you want to conquer fear, do not sit home and think about it. Go out and get busy."

– Dale Carnegie

As we work to cultivate a mindset for setting and achieving massive goals for ourselves, we have to talk about the role that fear plays in our lives. It's not the most enjoyable thing to talk about because so many of us (myself included) don't like to admit or even acknowledge our fears.

Fear can be a powerful emotion. When I see a snake, I receive a surge of fear-based adrenaline that I could probably use to lift a bus. I'm afraid of snakes, spiders, getting lost in the woods, falling from high places (not a fear of heights—a fear of falling), and so many other things.

We're all afraid of different things, and it's okay to admit that. The only way to move past a fear is to acknowledge it and work towards overcoming it. But sometimes we refuse to admit our fears to ourselves.

Sometimes, whether we know it or not, we change our inner narrative.

For example, maybe someone is afraid to learn how to swim. Perhaps he is afraid of drowning or looking silly while learning. Instead of admitting those fears, he says that swimming isn't something he's ever wanted to do. People invite him to pool parties or to the lake, and he declines, "Nah, I've never really been a fan of swimming. I've got other plans anyway."

As he tells himself this story over and over, he accepts this fictional tale over the truth: he is afraid of swimming, and he's afraid to admit it. Over time he begins to believe the new narrative he's told himself.

Could it be the same for goal setting?

As a huge fan of goal setting, it always stumps me when I talk to someone who says they don't like setting goals.

Perhaps you're one of those people, and until now, maybe you've told yourself that you don't like setting goals. Have you ever wondered why?

There have been so many studies on goal setting and the positive effects it has on people's success that, for me, it's undeniable: goal setting rocks! Yet, in spite of the research, many people still resist or avoid setting goals for themselves.

Why?!

I believe that people who avoid goal setting do so because they possess one of six different fears, and it's those fears that I want to explore in this chapter.

Maybe you don't think that you're afraid of goal setting, but please bear with me and keep reading. We often have fears that we've unknowingly buried or suppressed. Other times, we might have fears that we didn't even know we had.

If you're someone who's been resisting or avoiding goal setting, dive a little deeper and see if any of these fears resonate with you.

I promise; the best way to get past fear is to take a hard look at your fears and decide to face them head on. We're in this together. We're all afraid of something, but goal setting doesn't have to be one of those fears.

1. Fear of Loss

When we set huge goals for ourselves, we have to face the fear of loss. This fear is probably not one you've considered, and it may seem a little unclear, so I'll explain what I mean.

When we set a goal, we must lose something in order to achieve that goal. It could be loss of time as we work towards the goal, or it could be a way of life, as the goal creates profound changes in your life. The loss could be any number of things.

For some of us, the loss is obvious and easy to spot. For others, perhaps those who are avoiding goal setting, the loss could be a subconscious obstacle seeking to sabotage your success.

For a long time, I resisted taking massive action towards this book. I was chipping away at it slowly, between other tasks and priorities, but I wasn't making significant progress.

I didn't want to lose momentum on my blog. I had been writing a new post each week and didn't want to lose steam by shifting my focus to writing a book instead. Deeper than that, I was afraid that a break from the blog would result in a loss of readers.

The fear of loss runs deeper than you might think. If you

reread that paragraph, you'll see me make mention of loss three different times. At first, I had no idea that these fears were holding me back.

After I took some time to reflect on why I was making so little progress on my book, I discovered that I needed to prioritize either my blog or my book. It was when I realized that I needed to put my blog on hold that I discovered the fears I just listed above. Until then, they were completely hidden from view.

Let's look at a more universal example: losing weight. Most people who want to lose weight understand that proper diet and exercise is the only real way to achieve that goal. But instead they pour their faith into crash diets, magic pills, and fly-by-night workout programs.

Why?

Because in their minds, proper diet and exercise equals the loss of their favorite foods or their free time. There it is again: the fear of loss.

It may be difficult to admit, but many people resist the gym or taking time to meal prep because they don't want to lose out on another more-enjoyable activity such as TV or family time.

Equally painful to admit, many people resist dieting because they don't want to lose out on burgers and fries, pizza, or their favorite sweet treats. I'm guilty myself!

But here's the irony: the fear of losing something you have is keeping you from something you want.

The hard truth is, no matter your goal, it's almost always going to cost you something else. When we set goals, loss is inevitable. But even though it sounds like it, loss is not always a bad thing.

Overcome the Six Fears of Goal Setting

If you want to make ten times more money each year, you're most likely going to adopt a new lifestyle, and you're going to ditch the old one.

If you want a new, larger house, you're most likely going to sell the older, smaller one. If you want a new job—you get the idea: out with the old, in with the new.

Loss isn't always bad, and sometimes it isn't even real.

If you're afraid of loss, ask yourself this question: is what you want truly going to cost you what you have? If you go on a diet and join a gym, are you really going to lose all of your free time? Are you really going to have to cut out pizza altogether? Maybe. Maybe not.

Once you decide whether or not the costs are real, you have to decide if what you want is important enough to give up what you have.

If you're hesitating in joining the gym because you believe it will cost you your family time, could you skip the gym and find a hobby that would provide you with both exercise and family time? Or, could you get up earlier and work out before your family wakes up?

In the first option, you're giving up the gym, but you're still achieving your fitness and family goals through a shared activity. In the second option, you're giving up sleeping in to workout earlier in the morning. Either way, you're going to lose something in the process.

But this form of loss isn't something to be afraid of. If we look at this process closely, it's just a matter of weighing options and making choices. Is what you want important enough to give up what you have? Or, is what you have more important than what you thought you wanted?

Once you determine what's most important to you, you will

have automatically decided what's NOT important to you. This newfound clarity will allow you to move forward without the fear of loss because you will have decided what you're okay with giving up and what you're not okay with giving up.

Either way, you'll be able to move forward with confidence, clarity, and without the fear of loss.

2. Fear of Judgement and Rejection

The second fear is the fear of judgment and rejection. Have you ever set a goal for yourself only to have people laugh at it?

- ⊗ "That will never happen!"
- ⊗ "You could never do that!"
- ⊗ "That's totally unrealistic/insane/stupid/crazy!"

Have you ever told someone about one of your goals in the past and received a response like that?

If you're someone who's currently avoiding goal setting, you might have to think pretty far back, maybe even to your childhood, to recall a time when you received an adverse or judgmental reaction.

As a kid, maybe you wanted to be a famous musician, and people told you to get your head out of the clouds and focus on your homework. That advanced calculus isn't going to solve itself.

Maybe you wanted to be a doctor, and people told you that you didn't have good enough grades, weren't smart enough, or that the education would be too expensive.

Think as far back as you can. Have you ever told someone about a goal and received a negative reaction or maybe even some ridicule? If so, could it be that you've been avoiding goal setting today to avoid similar ridicule, judgment, and rejection?

Here's the deal, when you set a massive goal for yourself, there are going to be people who think it's impossible for you because they believe it's impossible for themselves, even if they don't consciously realize it or admit it.

Honestly, it's that simple.

Have you ever heard of projection? Projection is "an unconscious self-defense mechanism characterized by a person unconsciously attributing their personal issues onto someone or something else as a form of delusion and denial." [4]

Sound familiar?

Here's an example:

"What do you want to do when you grow up," Pete asked one of his more ambitious classmates?

"I've always loved standing up for people, so my goal is to graduate from law school with honors and become a defense attorney for less fortunate people," responded Alex assuredly.

Pete's eyes grew wide for a moment and then exclaimed, "Dude, do you have any idea how difficult law school is? It's hard enough just to get in, never mind getting good enough grades for honors. And how do you expect to make money working for poor people? You know you're going to have tons of student loan debt to pay off, right?"

In this example, Pete is projecting his insecurities onto Alex. Pete doesn't believe he has what it takes to achieve something as challenging as getting into or passing law school, so he can't comprehend Alex being able to do it either. Then to further plant a seed of doubt in Alex's mind, Pete implies that he'll never make money doing this job.

Now, I totally made this story up, but I've seen similar situations play out time and time again.

You may have been on the receiving end of a situation like this more than once in your life. It's difficult to admit, but you might have been in Pete's shoes a time or two as well, projecting self-doubt onto those around you. Who hasn't?

We all have doubts and fears, and when we see people doing big things, things we don't believe we could do ourselves, our inner voice starts shouting. And sometimes that inner voice spills over into what we say to other people.

Some people allow this negative internal dialog to go on for so long, that the things they tell themselves become part of their belief system and a part of who they are. They become resentful of people who take on big challenges and win. They begin to ridicule, judge, and reject people who appear to be more successful than they are themselves.

When this happens, these people, whether they know it or not, hope to hold you back. Subconsciously, they don't want to lose you, so they want to hold you back so that you can stay together.

That's fine; those people can stay where they are—there's nothing wrong with that, but if you aspire for more, then you should shoot for more. You don't have to feel bad for wanting to reach a new level in your own life.

Yes, people will judge you and call you crazy. Yes, reaching a new level might mean leaving those people behind—they may even reject or resent you for it. Sometimes growing into the person you want to become means outgrowing some of the people in your life.

You cannot allow people to place their doubts, fears, and limitations on you. You're meant for more. You're meant for great things. That's why you have dreams! You cannot allow the fear of judgment and rejection hold you back from your dreams and goals.

Do you worry about what people might think or say?

If so, I encourage you to set that crazy goal anyway. Make it huge! The crazier, the better! Darren Hardy says, "If you state your goal and they don't laugh, it's not big enough."

I agree! And here's the thing, you need to find a new group of people who will cheer you on instead of judge you and hold you back. Let me be your cheerleader. Shoot me an email or hit me up at www.dailynewyears.com. I'll support you and your goals no matter how crazy they sound!

But whatever you do, don't let the haters or naysayers destroy your goals or your spirits. You were meant for more!

3. Fear of Discontent

The fear of discontent is a fear that I encounter quite a bit. This fear comes from a noble and humble mindset, so it can be difficult to identify as a fear.

You see, setting goals for yourself means that you aspire to higher levels in life, and to aspire to higher levels means you don't like where you're at in life. Right?

This idea is one that my wife, Callie, and I debate from time to time. She's content with life, and she's grateful for everything we have. You will honestly never find someone more grateful and humble than my wife. I'm so blessed to have her in my life and in my corner.

Me on the other hand? I'm always shooting for the next level. As soon as I've achieved one thing, I'm on to the next. I have massive goals for my life. However, like my wife, I'm grateful for everything we have. We're blessed beyond belief, and I know it! On that much, she and I can agree.

However, sometimes she's afraid that, by shooting for more, we might end up feeling ungrateful and discontent with what we have. It's a valid concern to be sure. It would be far too easy to fall into the trap of never being satisfied with life.

I'm just not convinced that ambition and goal setting lead to feelings of discontent. Personally, I don't believe that aspiring to new levels means that you don't appreciate your current level in life or that goal setting is a gateway drug to discontent. I believe that goal setting is how we grow as people—it's how we reach new levels in our lives. It's not just about getting a bigger house, a fancier car, or a larger, thinner TV. Heck no!

Goal setting is about pushing yourself to be better—to be a better spouse, a better parent, a better boss or employee, a better version of you, and so on. It's about being Better Every Day!

If you're not setting goals because you're worried that you'll seem dissatisfied with your life or that you'll be walking down a path of discontent, please consider this: You did not get where you are today by sitting still as a young child. You had goals before you knew what goals were, you worked hard to reach new levels, and you succeeded. You most likely learned to walk, swim, and ride a bike without training wheels. Those were some of your goals before you knew what goals were.

You got where you are today because, at some point, you wanted more and you went for it. But if that's no longer true, what changed? When did you decide that you had achieved enough?

At some point, perhaps you reached a comfortable spot in your life, and you stopped pushing yourself forward, and you stopped setting goals.

But what still lies ahead for you in life? How many years do you think you have left to live? Ten? Twenty? Fifty? Are you okay with staying where you are as a person, never growing or improving, for the rest of your life?

You can be thankful for your life and everything you have and still want more. That's okay because you're not done growing as a person. You have so much further to go.

How will you know what you were meant to be if you stay where you are? How will you know where your potential ends if you never seek to find it?

There's nothing wrong with aspiring to higher levels in life—it's how we grow and become the people we were born to be. Don't confuse ambition with dissatisfaction or discontent. As long as you remain grateful and humble along the way, it's okay to want more from life.

So go ahead, step forward into your greatness—set some goals for yourself and see what kind of life you were truly meant to live.

4. Fear of the Unknown

Next up: fear of the unknown. I put this fear close to the middle because the first three fears seem to manifest in people who actively avoid and resist goal setting. As you'll soon see, the last two fears tend to manifest in people who want to set goals but are afraid of what might come next. The unknown is the void that falls somewhere in the middle.

I encounter many people who don't set goals because they don't know what they want or where they're going. Not only do they not know where they're going, but they're afraid that they might go in the wrong direction, so instead, they sit still.

> "If I pursue A, I may not get to do B. But if I do

> B, I may not get to do C. And what about options D-Z!"

The fear of choosing the wrong path can be paralyzing. Everywhere you look and every option you weigh only seems to provide more questions and what-ifs.

The lack of clarity can be overwhelming, even stressful to the point of driving you to stay where you are. If everywhere you look is more of the unknown, it's easier to stay put. At least you're familiar with where you are, right?

Wrong!

If you want more in life, you have to understand that doing nothing is a short path to nowhere and it's a path that will get you there pretty fast.

Any Path is Better than No Path

If you're actively looking at multiple options for your future, clearly you want more for yourself. You want to try something new. You want to reach higher levels. The problem is that you just don't know which new thing or which higher level to aim for.

I would suggest that if you have a lot of different dreams for your future—simply pick one and try it. Something is better than nothing!

Set a goal and start down a path. Any path!

If it's the wrong one, you will have learned something new about yourself. You can move on to the next thing with confidence that you're closer to the right path. You'll never have to look back and wonder "what if?"

On the other hand, if you can't bring yourself to pick a path and just hope for the best, do some Blue-Sky Thinking and picture your life twenty-five years from now.

Blue-Sky Thinking

If you've never heard of Blue-Sky Thinking, here's how to do it:

Imagine you had absolutely no limits. You could do anything, be anything, and go anywhere you wanted. What would you do? Where would you go? What would your life look like as a whole? Blue-Sky Thinking is a great way to start with the end in mind. We'll dive deeper into this concept in chapter 6.

If you can picture where your dream life is going to end up, you can start setting goals and planning for that future today. You can overcome the unknown and move forward with clarity.

I used to have an internal struggle between several career options that I had in front of me. Once I did my own Blue-Sky Thinking session, I was able to end my internal conflict. I imagined my dream life and picked a path towards that dream. After that, my goals began falling into place.

You may have a dozen options or opportunities that you want to pursue. Maybe they all take you beyond your comfort zone and into the unknown. That very situation may be causing you to sit still, but what single goal can you set today that will move you forward towards the life you want?

Identify that one goal and step bravely out into the unknown.

5. Fear of Failure

I bet you didn't see this one coming, did you? Yes, the fear of failure is probably the most common fear that holds people back from their goals.

- "What if I fail?"
- "What if I'm not good enough?"
- "What if I'm not smart enough?"
- "What if I find out my dreams are unattainable?"

We get so wrapped up in the what-ifs that we give up on trying altogether, and this isn't always a deliberate choice. Sometimes the fear of failure sneaks up on us.

Maybe you've tried something big in the past, and it didn't go as planned. Perhaps it was embarrassing, so you slowly and quietly stopped setting goals to avoid embarrassment. This phenomenon is our brain's natural way of defending us against painful and unpleasant feelings.

Perhaps you took a significant risk on a goal, and it had adverse effects on your life. Maybe you started a business and lost a large sum of money or went bankrupt.

The fear of failure is not one we're born with; it's one we learn along the way. If you're afraid of failure, then it most likely comes from past experience, whether that's yours or someone else's close to you. When we see the damage that failure can do, we start conditioning our minds to avoid similar situations for ourselves.

Over time, we can build a pretty big defensive network that protects us from failure. At the core of that defense is one key idea: I can't fail if I don't try.

You Can't Fail if You Don't Try

When we try and fail over and over, we subconsciously come to realize that we can stop failing if we stop trying. This causes us to stick close to our comfort zones. When we don't try, we can always use the old cop-out, "I could have done that if I had wanted to, but [insert some excuse here]."

"I could have become a doctor; I just didn't want to spend that much time in school."

"I could have been in the NFL. I just hated going to practice."

It's easier to convince ourselves that we could have, had we tried, than it is to try and fail, whether the former is true or not. Sure, I can agree that you cannot fail if you do not try, but you can't succeed either. So if you can't succeed by sitting still, isn't sitting still also a form of failing?

If so, why not go ahead and try something new and learn along the way?

John Maxwell has a book called *Sometimes You Win—Sometimes You Learn: Life's Greatest Lessons Are Gained from Our Losses*. I'll give you one guess as to what that book is about.

The title is an adaptation from the old saying, "Sometimes you win. Sometimes you lose," and the book is about turning life's failures into your greatest learning opportunities.

You Can't Lose if You Choose to Learn Instead

I believe that in life, you only lose or fail when you've accepted failure as the final outcome. I believe that in every failure, there is a lesson to be learned. So if you're afraid to set a goal because you might fail, set that goal anyway.

If you do fail, look for the lesson, overcome it, and then try again. (More on this in chapter 14.)

Henry Ford once said, "Failure is only the opportunity to more intelligently begin again."

There's also an old adage that says, "Courage is not the absence of fear, but moving forward in spite of it."

You only fail when you've quit, and you're not a quitter; you're a Goal Getter. Remember, as long as you're trying, you're winning. You've got this!

6. Fear of Success

The sixth and final fear that keeps people from setting goals is the fear of success.

You might be thinking, "What? Huh? The whole point of setting goals is to succeed! This doesn't make any sense!"

Sure it does! You see, when we try and fail, we can retreat to our comfort zones. When we fail, we can go back to the things we know. That's not so bad, is it?

If you're trying to turn a side hustle into a full-time career and it fails, you can keep working at your current job, right? Of course you can! No harm done.

But what if we succeed?

When we succeed we have to move into the unknown realm of success. There's no way to know what life will look like if we succeed, and if you ask me, that can be far scarier than dealing with failure!

The problem with fearing success is that it's a tough fear to recognize or understand, and that makes it difficult to overcome. That's why we're going to take a look at how to recognize and deal with this fear, starting with the Upper Limit Problem.

The Upper Limit Problem

Author Gay Hendricks wrote a fantastic book called *The Big Leap*. In it, he talks about overcoming what he calls the Upper Limit Problem.

The Upper Limit Problem is when we subconsciously sabotage ourselves when we're about to achieve a new level of success in our lives that we're not mentally or emotionally ready to handle.

In his book, he says that we all have internal, hidden limitations from years of conditioned beliefs. Deep down, we may not believe that we can attain a higher level of success, so any time we come close, we sabotage ourselves. Essentially, the Upper Limit Problem is the fear of success.

Here's a great example: Someday I want to be the CEO of a successful company. As much as I want to be CEO someday, I don't fully know what working as a CEO is like, or what it's going to mean for my life.

I imagine it will bring some new stress into my life, but my overall perception is that I'm equipped for the job and will do it well. However, it's still scary as heck to think about the pressures that might come with the role!

If I succeed in obtaining the position, I'll be responsible for growing the business, sustaining profits, enriching lives, and so much more. If I succeed in becoming the CEO, my life is going to change in a significant way! For many, this fear could activate the Upper Limit Problem and the self sabotage that comes with it.

Fortunately, I've learned to spot the fear of success through various books and articles that I've read over the years, so I don't plan on allowing the fear of success or the Upper Limit Problem to stop me from shooting for my goals. I've concluded that, if I want to shoot for new levels in life, I have to deal with the discomfort that each new level brings, and you will, too.

Leveling Up in Life

Leveling up in life is like leveling up in a video game—each time you get a better weapon or a new skill, the bad guys suddenly get harder to beat.

If you're a gamer, you know what I mean. Each time you reach a new level, you have to work extra hard to get back to your previous level of comfort. And as soon as you do, the game forces you to level up again.

When we stay at the same level, life becomes almost effortless. Think about the last time you reached a new level in your life. It was hard at first, right?

I remember when I was sixteen, and I got my first job at McDonald's as a cook. Everyone could assemble the sandwiches so quickly and effortlessly, and I thought that I would never be able to keep up with them.

I was wrong—way wrong. I worked hard and forced myself to learn as quickly as I could. I was uncomfortable at first, but I wanted to be the fastest. It was difficult, but I've always been competitive. So in just a few short weeks, I had the job down pat and it only required minimal effort. In spite of the discomfort, I leveled up.

Another time in my life that springs to mind is transitioning from high school to college. As a high school senior, things were easy. You have the building memorized, you know how much effort your classes take, and you know just about everyone around you. Then you go to college. The campus is huge, buildings are everywhere, classes are way harder, and you don't know anyone. But then, by senior year, everything is easy-breezy again. You level up.

If you think back, there have been countless times where you have reached a new level in your life, too, times where you rose to the occasion. It was uncomfortable at first but then became easier. Take a second and try to think of some times like that in your life. No, really. Take a second to bask in your past successes.

As we look at goal setting, we can see it's the same thing. When we set huge goals for ourselves, we're aiming for higher levels in life. Don't fear it. Instead, acknowledge it and embrace the struggle. New goals are going to be challenging at first, but they'll get easier as time goes on. And when they start getting easier, it will be time to set new, harder goals all over again. You've done it before, and you can do it again.

Overcoming Your Fears

Now that you've read up on the six fears of goal setting, do any of them resonate with you? Is there one that seems to resonate more than the others? For me, it's the fear of failure.

Perhaps several of them resonate with you, and that's okay! The first step in overcoming your fear is acknowledging it. Once you do that, you can begin to understand it, learn about it, and even conquer its control over you. The more you learn about your fear, the easier it will be to overcome.

Whatever you do, don't bury your head in the sand and succumb to your fears. Strive to overcome them and set massive goals for your life.

Using the exercises in the workbook, attempt to identify which of these six fears might be holding you back and use the corresponding worksheets to begin working through those fears.

As much as you may want to, don't skip this step. In the next chapter, we're going to be learning how to improve our self-confidence in goal setting, and we can't have fear hold us back.

Good luck! I'll see you in the next chapter.

CHAPTER RECAP

Key Takeaways

- **We're all afraid of something**; that's completely normal. The only way to move past a fear is to acknowledge it and work towards overcoming it.
- **Some fears are subconscious** and are difficult to identify. Take a hard look within and reflect deeply to identify what your fears may be and then try to summon the courage to face them head on.
- The first step in overcoming fear is to acknowledge it. Once you do that, you can begin to understand it, learn about it, and even master it.

The Six Fears of Goal Setting are:

- **Fear of Loss**
  We all fear losing something: time, friends, opportunities, a way of life, security, stability; it could be anything. But not all loss is bad. You have to ask, "Is what I'm going to gain worth what I'm going to lose?" If it is, set that goal and go all in.

- **Fear of Judgment and Rejection**
  Is postponing your dreams worth avoiding judgment? Don't avoid goal setting to prevent ridicule, judgment, or rejection. Find a group of people who will cheer you on instead of judge you and hold you back. Set a goal and chase your dreams.

- **Fear of Discontent**
  Goal setting is how we grow as people—it's how we reach new levels in our lives. It's possible to want more in life and set goals for yourself AND be grateful and happy for what you have at the same time.

Overcome the Six Fears of Goal Setting

- **Fear of the Unknown**
  Doing nothing is a short path to nowhere, and it will get you there pretty fast. Any path is better than no path, and forward motion is better than no motion. Use Blue-Sky Thinking to help plan your future and step forward with clarity.

- **Fear of Failure**
  You only fail when you've accepted failure as a final outcome. Instead, take a chance on your dreams. If you miss the mark, seize the opportunity to learn and begin again more intelligently, but never give up.

- **Fear of Success**
  If you think back over your life, there have been countless times where you have reached a new level in your life and ventured beyond your comfort zone. It was uncomfortable at first but it became easier with time. The next level of is no different.

Memorable Quotes

- *"If you state your goal and they don't laugh, it's not big enough."* —Darren Hardy

- *"Failure is only the opportunity to more intelligently begin again."* —Henry Ford

- *"Courage is not the absence of fear, but moving forward in spite of it."*

Put it into Practice

- Use the corresponding worksheets to identify your fears and begin working towards overcoming them.

How to Build Rock-Solid Self-Confidence

"Each time we face our fear, we gain strength, courage and confidence in the doing."
– Theodore Roosevelt.

Pop quiz: How would you rate yourself in the area of self-confidence?

That's a tricky question, isn't it? I mean, when it comes to dancing in public or singing karaoke, my self-confidence is practically zero! I don't want anything to do with those activities!

Self-confidence can vary throughout the different areas of our lives, though, so I'll revise my question. Because we're working towards developing a Goal Getter's mindset, how confident are you in your ability to achieve your goals?

When you set a goal, do you begin with pre-planted seeds of doubt in your mind? In your mind, have you failed before you've even started? Or do you know, without a shadow of a doubt, that you're going to crush it? Are you somewhere in between?

Before we move onto specific goal-setting strategies, it's imperative that we establish and reinforce your confidence around the areas of success and goal setting.

The Relationship Between Self-Discipline, Self-Confidence, and Self-Esteem

When we explore the idea of self-confidence in goal setting, we can often connect it with our self-esteem and our self-discipline. The three areas are closely related. When we improve our self-discipline, our self-confidence goes up. When our self-confidence goes up, so does our self-esteem. The cycle is like an upward spiral that carries us higher in life.

Have you ever heard of a thermal column? Essentially, a thermal column (or thermal) is "a column of rising air in the lower altitudes of Earth's atmosphere, a form of atmospheric updraft. Thermals are created by the uneven heating of Earth's surface from solar radiation." [5]

Eagles and other birds are able to use these thermals to gain altitude by simply gliding in circles as the warm air carries them upward. These birds may have to work hard to get into the thermal but once inside, they can climb almost effortlessly.

This metaphor has never been more accurate than it is with self-discipline, self-confidence, and self-esteem. As you work to improve these three areas of your life, you will be able to rise more easily over time.

You see, when we set goals, we have to practice self-discipline to see them through to completion. When we do that, we gain some self-confidence in our ability to achieve our other goals. As we continue crushing our goals, our confidence builds and builds, and we climb higher and higher with reduced effort each time. All the while, our self-esteem as a whole begins to soar!

This isn't a new idea. I reference Brian Tracy's book, Goals! a lot on my blog, and I wanted to mention a brief message from his book here as well.

In chapter 12, Brian says,

> "Whenever you practice self-discipline in the pursuit of your goals, your self-esteem goes up. Whenever you force yourself to persist in the face of temptation or adversity, you like and respect yourself more."
>
> "As your self-esteem increases and you like yourself more, your ability to discipline yourself increases as well. Each exercise of self-discipline builds your self-esteem, which, in return, increases your self-discipline." [6]

What Mr. Tracy says is true!

When you commit to one small goal and achieve it, you build self-confidence within yourself that screams, "You've got this!" Then you set another goal, and you carry that positive energy into the next goal, and then the next.

On and on it goes, goal after goal, your self-confidence grows. Eventually, you begin to feel unstoppable.

I always knew that achieving goal after goal was a great way to build momentum and achieve greater success, but I never realized how good the momentum made me feel about myself until I started to struggle with my goals and my momentum began to fall apart.

Self-Discipline Begets Self-Discipline

A year ago, I was riding an upward spiral and didn't even realize it. I started my blog, and I was working on it every day. I was going to the gym five days a week. I had a routine, and I was killing it—until I wasn't. As I got busier and busier with goals that seemed to be competing with each other, I began cutting things from my daily routine.

After I stopped going to the gym, I stopped drinking my morning protein shakes. Then because I skipped a healthy breakfast, I started eating unhealthy lunches and having a beer or two with dinner every night.

Drinking a couple of beers every night caused me to stay up later and sleep in longer. My morning goals suffered, I became more tired, and a cycle of bad habits began to set in.

I realized that self-discipline begets more self-discipline. The more things I did to support my goals, the easier it was to maintain all of those things—they were linked. That's why the upward spiral worked so well. However, I also realized that the opposite was also true: lack of self-discipline leads to even less self-discipline.

It seems that the more I compromised, the easier compromising became. Cutting one good thing lead to cutting another good thing. My self-discipline was crumbling, and so was my confidence in my ability to crush my goals. I began spiraling back down, and it didn't feel good. The worst part was, I almost didn't realize it was happening.

Compromising Our Self-Confidence

Perhaps this very thing has happened to you.

How many times have you tried to lose weight, stop drinking, quit smoking, or break some other not-so-great habit?

How to Build Rock-Solid Self-Confidence

You start by counting the days: "I've been seven days without a cigarette."

Because you've tried before and failed, you're pretty sure you can't quit altogether, right? And since you can't quit altogether (in your mind), you decide to see how long you can go before you eventually fail. "Hey, I made it 24 days this time. New record!"

Maybe you don't smoke, but I think you can relate to what I'm saying here.

When we have a track record of failing, we resort to counting the days that we do succeed because our self-confidence and our self-discipline are too low to help us achieve the real success we want. We make compromises with ourselves with the hope of feeling better, but it doesn't work. Without even realizing it, we're damaging our confidence and our self-esteem.

And it's not just breaking bad habits—it's achieving our goals, too.

So many people set goals to become debt-free, to save money, to run a half-marathon, to go on a European vacation, to learn a new skill, or [insert your dream goal here].

Whatever it is, when we set a goal and give up on it, we're telling ourselves that we're not good enough to achieve our goals. Every time we try and fail, our self-confidence plummets further, and eventually we stop trying altogether.

But it doesn't have to be that way! If we can start winning some small battles, we can begin restoring our self-confidence, and we can begin to build ourselves back up.

Fortunately, I realized what was happening to me when my routine began to disintegrate. I knew something was off. I knew my routine was in shambles and that I was underperforming with my goals.

Fortunately, my self-confidence hadn't fallen too far in the short time my routine fell apart, so I forced myself to snap out of it. I told myself to get it together, and I worked towards rebooting my routine. (I love a good routine! We'll talk more about routines in chapter 11.)

But maybe your self-confidence has taken a severe beating over the years. Or maybe, you didn't have a lot of confidence to begin with due to the way you were raised or the influences you had growing up. If that's the case, let's take a look at seven tips for improving your self-confidence.

7 Tips for Improving Self-Confidence

When your self-confidence is low, especially around goal setting, the best way to give yourself a boost is by working towards better self-discipline and an improved mindset.

Here are seven tips for doing exactly that.

1. Get Plenty of Sleep—No Matter What

As you may already know, willpower, motivation, and decision-making are finite resources. We have a limited supply of each that runs out every day, so we need to make sure to use them wisely. More importantly, we need to get plenty of sleep so that we can recharge.

When we're tired, we tend to make poor decisions more frequently. When this happens, we tend to spiral out of control. One compromise leads to another, and before you know it, your discipline is off the rails, and your goals are a distant memory.

A good night's sleep will allow you to start your day off with a positive mindset and a full tank of willpower and decision-making fuel. Always get plenty of sleep—no matter what.

2. Prioritize Your Goals

One of the quickest ways to run your discipline straight into the ground is wearing yourself out by chasing a thousand different things. To stay disciplined and achieve your goals, you have to prioritize your own goals first, when possible.

When you make time for yourself first, you're telling yourself that you're most important and that you're number one. That's good!

In doing so, you're allowing yourself to work on your most meaningful goals, and you boost your self-confidence in the process. Working towards your own goals before everyone else's is energizing, and you're going to want to chase that feeling. (This sounds selfish, but hang with me.)

On the other hand, when you make time for everyone else's goals above your own, you will start to feel "less than." When you don't prioritize your goals, other people won't either. They will layer on more tasks and projects until you grow resentful.

You might begin to think, "How can they not see I have my own things to do? Don't they understand that my needs are important too?"

It can be challenging to prioritize yourself without disregarding the people around you, especially if you're in a caretaker role. I doubt you would want to ditch your responsibilities as a mother, father, spouse, employee, or any other role you might be filling. I certainly didn't want to let my wife down while I was writing this book, so I didn't drop my duties as a husband.

It's good to be helpful when it comes to other people, especially at work, but it takes a delicate balance. I'm not suggesting that you err on the side of selfishness and only make time for yourself, but you also can't allow your time to get swallowed up by everyone else.

If you want to crush your goals and feel more self-confident, don't be afraid or ashamed to prioritize yourself when needed. Everyone deserves to make themselves a priority. You'll feel better knowing that you made some time for yourself and the people around you will grow to respect you more for it. Win-win.

3. Learn to Say, "No!"

Prioritizing your goals isn't always enough—there are always going to be other people presenting you with countless opportunities.

Remember, we're trying to build our self-discipline and self-confidence. We want to know that we can achieve our own goals, and to do that, you have to defend your goals and the time it takes to achieve them.

Saying no can be difficult, but just like with anything else, practice makes perfect. Anytime you're presented with an opportunity, ask yourself if this new opportunity is going to derail your goals. If it will, permit yourself to decline.

As you achieve more of your goals, your self-confidence will grow and saying, "No!" will become more comfortable—I promise.

4. Build a Routine

Over the years, I've realized that I'm at my strongest when I'm in my routine. Life can be hard, and some days require more motivation and willpower than others. A daily routine is the best thing for getting you through the more difficult days.

When you examine your goals, try to break them down into the smallest pieces possible, then attempt to build habits and routines around those goals.

I love to learn about high performance and personal development, and reading books is a great way to learn those things. However, reading isn't one of my favorite pastimes. To overcome this, I built a daily reading goal to stay on track.

Getting started took a lot of self-discipline, but once I built the routine, autopilot kept me going. This routine comes in handy on days where I'm feeling too worn out or unmotivated to read.

And it doesn't stop there! I've built routines around writing, podcasting, working out, and more. What routines can you create to support your goals and improve your self-confidence?

5. Embrace the Confidence/Competence Loop

I'm a huge fan of Brendon Burchard, author of *High Performance Habits*, *Life's Golden Ticket*, *The Charge*, and several other books. One of his teachings is the confidence/competence loop. It goes like this: the more you learn about a topic, the more confident you become in that area.

Want to be a confident chef? Read, watch, listen, and learn as much as you can about cooking techniques, ingredients, recipes, and so on.

Want to be a master goal-setter? Learn as much as you can on the subject. Hey, you're already doing that, and I've got mad respect for you for it!

Essentially, the more you learn in any topic, the more confident you become in that area. As your confidence goes up, the more likely you are to continue pursuing that topic.

Going back to the master chef example, as you learn and begin to feel more confident, you might decide to start cooking for friends and family. There, you will undoubtedly learn a great deal and get a strong dose of encouragement. As your confidence and competence grow, you'll begin to take on larger, scarier cooking engagements, such as paid dinner parties. As you do so, you'll continue to learn more advanced aspects of cooking.

Regardless of what you're aiming to do, understand that the more you learn about it, the more confident you can become in that area.

6. Acknowledge Your Adequacy

The feeling of inadequacy is the opposite of self-confidence. Wait—did you catch that? Read that again. The feeling of inadequacy is the opposite of self-confidence.

When we feel inadequate, we don't feel good enough. One of the biggest reasons people don't set goals is due to not feeling good enough to achieve them.

But here's the truth: you *are* good enough. The fact that you're here, reading this book, means that you have the right mindset to achieve massive success in your life. You may lack the self-confidence to see yourself for who you really are, but I promise you this: you have what it takes!

What you know right now is more than enough to get you started towards achieving your goals. You just have to get started. The journey of a thousand miles begins with one step. Embrace your adequacy and take the first step.

7. Take Massive Action

The last tip I'm going to give you for building your self-confidence is one that you're going to see throughout this book because it's mission critical. You need to take massive action towards your goals.

Yes, taking action can be scary, but waking up in the same place in your life fifty years from now is even more terrifying. Wouldn't you agree?

As much as I try not to be, I'm relatively risk averse. The idea of taking significant risks usually stops me from starting big things. However, one of Brendon Burchard's High-Performance Coaches helped me to realize that there is just as much risk in sitting still as there is in taking action. You risk stagnation, never seeing your dreams come true, and you even risk your future.

Please don't stay where you are!

Take action towards your dreams. I always say that starting small, taking action, and building momentum are the biggest keys to success in any endeavor, and that includes building discipline, confidence, and self-esteem.

You can't build confidence in your life or in your ability to crush your goals if you don't take action first.

Choosing Your Destination

We're all on a journey, and we're all headed for a destination. Some of us are deciding on the destination and planning our route. Others, however, have no idea where they're going.

Some aren't even aware they're on a journey, and someday they're going to wake up in a place that they don't recognize or enjoy.

Which of these sounds like you?

Are you going to sit in the passenger's seat and see where life takes you? Or are you going to take the wheel and choose your own destination?

If you've taken anything away from this chapter, I hope it's this: discipline, confidence, and self-esteem are directly connected, and if you want to crush your biggest goals in life, you have to work towards improving all three. You're in control of how you feel.

Remember: discipline begets discipline. The more you practice it, the better you'll get at it and the easier it will become. Your confidence in your ability to achieve massive goals will soar, and you'll be practically unstoppable.

We're very close to diving into practical, hands-on goal-setting strategies. We've explored how to find our why, how to overcome our fears, and how to build our self-confidence, but there's one more element that's crucial to our long-term, goal-setting foundation, and that's our mindset.

In the next chapter, we're going to take a close look at nine different philosophies, or belief systems, that will help reframe our perspective for a lifetime of successful goal setting. But before we move on, take some time and use exercises in the workbook to reflect on your current self-confidence, self-discipline, and self-esteem, and to craft a plan for improving all three.

How to Build Rock-Solid Self-Confidence

CHAPTER RECAP

Key Takeaways

- **Self-discipline** and **self-confidence** are connected. When we practice discipline and achieve a goal, our confidence in our ability to crush our other goals goes up as well.
- Self-discipline leads to more self-discipline but the opposite is also true. When we **make compromises** with ourselves, it only gets easier to make more compromises.
- To stay disciplined and achieve your goals, you have to **prioritize your own goals first**. When you make time for yourself first, you're telling yourself that you're most important—that you're number one. That's good!
- Brendon Burchard's **confidence/competence loop** states that the more you learn about a topic, the more confident you become in that area. You can reinforce your confidence in crushing your goals by learning as much as you can about them.
- The **feeling of inadequacy** is the opposite of self-confidence. One of the biggest reasons people don't set goals is due to not feeling good enough to achieve them. You have what it takes!
- You can't build confidence in your life or in your ability to crush your goals if you don't take **massive action**.
- Are you going to sit in the passenger's seat and see where life takes you? Or are you going to take the wheel and **choose your own destination**?

Memorable Quotes

☆ *"Whenever you practice self-discipline in the pursuit of your goals, your self-esteem goes up."* —Brian Tracy

☆ *"The journey of a thousand miles begins with one step."* —Chinese proverb.

Put it into Practice

☐ Spend one week working towards building your self-discipline by following these steps:
   1. **Get plenty of sleep** and recharge your willpower nightly.
   2. **Prioritize yourself** by working towards your goals first each day.
   3. **Say "No!" more often.** This week (and beyond) make time for your goals first. Only say yes to things you truly want to do. Say no to everything that will distract you from your goals.
   4. **Start building a routine** around the success of your goals. Automating your goals is a great way to reinforce your self-discipline.
   5. **Embrace the confidence/competence loop.** This week, learn as much as you can on topics that support your active goals.
   6. **Acknowledge your adequacy** by telling yourself that you are good enough to achieve your goals. Journal it daily!
   7. **Take massive action** towards your goals daily. For one week, do as much as you can each day to crush your goals.

↪ Complete the corresponding worksheets and self-assessments to begin improving your self-confidence and self-discipline.

Develop a Goal Getter's Mindset

"It's hard to beat a person who never gives up."
– Babe Ruth

So far in this section we've covered some deep topics, wouldn't you agree? We've explored how having a strong why is paramount for long-term goal setting. We've faced our fears head on and we've began to work towards building our self-confidence. I don't want to come across as condescending, but given what we've covered so far, I'm super proud of you! Taking a hard look in the mirror and examining your mindset is both brave and incredibly difficult.

As you work your way through this book, there's no denying that you'll be challenged in several ways, especially when it comes to your mindset. I want to go beyond the obvious advice and typical inspirational quotes that commonly come along with the topic of mindset. We'll still leave room for some of that throughout the book because every now and then that's what we might need. However, the main focus of this chapter is to highlight and explore a few important mindsets, or beliefs, that will aid you on your journey.

When most people approach goal setting, they focus on the strategies and techniques first and often skip over developing a success-oriented mindset. As you'll see throughout this book, I believe that strategies and techniques are essential (we're jumping into those in the next section!), but I believe that having the right mindset trumps everything else.

As much as you may want to skip this chapter and jump straight into the *fun* stuff, I encourage you to take your time with this chapter. Having the proper mindset is the rock-solid foundation on which to build your goal-setting success. The last thing you would want to do is build a house in the sand, right?

As aspiring Goal Getters, we need to challenge our current belief systems and thought patterns. We need to rewire our brains and unlearn any negative belief systems that may attempt to hold us back down the road.

In this chapter, we're going to examine the Goal Getter's mindset. We're going to take a close look at how high-achieving Goal Getters think so that we can begin to recondition our own mindsets for maximum success and achievement.

Please don't read the following nine concepts as you must possess these characteristics to proceed. That's not the idea here at all. I don't want to discourage you—I want to be your coach as you work towards honing your mindset.

In reading this chapter, you may find that you possess some of these characteristics. Others, you may not (yet). Either way, these beliefs can be learned, practiced, and refined. Whether you believe in these ideas or not, I want to invite you to explore them with me because I believe they will help you along the way.

If you're ready, let's dive in.

1. The Better Every Day Mindset

The Better Every Day mindset is the foundational mindset of anyone seeking to crush their goals. As you begin setting goals for yourself, it's important to understand that it's not always going to be sunshine and rainbows.

Some days, your goals may not go as planned. It's true; stuff happens. Things come up and sometimes life gets in the way. There may be days that you make massive progress towards your goals, followed by several days of no progress at all.

I've been there.

Other days, you may experience a setback that feels like ten steps in the wrong direction.

Yeah, I've been there, too.

It can be frustrating, but the Better Every Day mindset means that as long as you're trying, you're getting better, and as long as you're getting better, you're winning.

In an interview on my Daily New Year's Podcast, blogger Elyse Lyons (aka The Savvy Sagittarius) said, "Goals aren't about being perfect; they're about being better than you were before." [1]

As soon as she said it, the thought became my new favorite quote!

---

[1] To listen to my interview with Elyse Lyons, The Savvy Sagittarius, visit www.dailynewyears.com/podcast and search "Elyse Lyons".

Sure, you're going to have bad days here and there—days where you feel stuck in place. But if you've been charging forward, chasing your dreams, and pursuing your goals, then at least you're not stuck at the beginning. You started something, and that's more than a lot of people can say.

So before you go any further, try to let go of your expectations and preconceived notions and embrace the idea that becoming Better Every Day is about progress, not perfection.

As long as you're trying, you're winning.

2. The Lifelong Learner Mindset

When you work towards becoming Better Every Day, you inevitably find yourself wanting to learn. Whether it's learning a relaxing new hobby, how to start investing, or how to start your own business, learning tends to come with the goal-setting territory.

In 2017, I came up with the idea for my blog, Daily New Year's, and I suddenly found myself learning how to work with WordPress and how to optimize my content so that people just like you could discover and enjoy the information. I found myself with a brand new thirst for learning about digital marketing, building a community on social media, proper writing strategy, and so much more.

When the blog launched, the learning didn't stop. To keep the blog ripe with new content, I had to keep discovering, reading, and learning about new ideas in the personal development space. When it comes to my goals, learning is absolutely essential.

Think about the last health or fitness goal you set for yourself (assuming you've set one at some point). Did you have to learn about a new diet or exercise? My money's on yes. If you've set a goal to buy your first house before, did you start out knowing what to do, or did you have to learn about home loans, insurance, remodeling, property taxes, and so on?

Goals are all about growth. The point of any goal is to achieve something new, to reach a new level, or to obtain something that you don't already have. And if goals are all about growth, then education is critical to the process, and it's okay to start out knowing nothing about a topic.

Any time we take on new goals, big or small, we need to approach them with a lifelong learner's mindset. When we believe that we've arrived, that we've become an expert, or that we've learned everything we need to learn, our growth is immediately stunted.

So if you don't already have a lifelong learner's mindset, be sure to work on developing one today. Start by listing out things that you're currently interested in. Did you have any childhood interests that you never pursued? Write those down, too. What are some things that you've always wanted to learn more about, but could never find the time? Be sure to add those to the list.

Do any of these things line up with your goals or could you set some goals around the things you want to learn?

If so, start listening to audiobooks, or subscribing to educational podcasts and YouTube channels, or reading for ten to fifteen minutes per day. Once you connect your goals with your interests, becoming a lifelong learner is a blast!

Because you're reading this book, you might be thinking, "I'm already trying to learn—that's why I bought this book."

Yes, you're reading this book, and I'm forever grateful for that, but as much as I want this to be the last book you ever need for becoming a high-achieving Goal Getter, this book can't be where your learning ends. As soon as you complete the final chapter I hope you'll jump headfirst into setting massive, long-term goals for yourself. Over time, though, you might need to revisit this book, or you might want to explore new goal-setting strategies via a blog or a podcast. Or you might need to learn specific skills to help you achieve your goals. That's fantastic!

As you embark on this goal-setting journey, prepare yourself for a life rich in learning. It might be frustrating from time to time, but embrace the process, enjoy it, and never stop learning.

3. The Positivity and Perseverance Mindset

Let's be honest: as much as goal setting can change our lives for the better, it's not always a walk down Easy Street. Right?

Yes, setting goals can transform your life in powerful ways, but it comes with a certain amount of struggle, too. I don't want to cast an illusion that goal setting will transform every aspect of your life into a wonderfully positive experience where you get everything you've ever dreamed of. I'm sorry. It won't.

I used to watch each year pass by as I waited for a new year to begin. "Next year will be my year," I would think to myself. "Next year, I will stick to my resolutions." I grew impatient with how slowly the things in my life were progressing, and I decided to set some goals for myself instead.

Today I no longer sit on the sidelines of my own life—I take charge. I set huge goals, and I try to crush them every day. But it's hard work. Some days I feel like I have the energy of a thousand suns. Other days, I feel like I need to take a month-long break and come back recharged and ready to start over.

This roller coaster ride of self-improvement comes with a lot of ups and downs, both physically and emotionally, so it would be pretty easy to become discouraged, overwhelmed, and exhausted. It would be pretty easy to succumb to the low points and quit altogether. But this is precisely why, as Goal Getters, we have to maintain a positive mindset and focus on perseverance.

We can't passively accept positivity when it comes—we have to generate positivity within ourselves. When I'm having a particularly rough time, I remind myself that it's in the turbulent times that we grow the most. When I'm especially tired, I remind myself that being tired is a good sign of how hard I've been working towards my dreams.

When I'm facing new challenges, or I'm having a difficult time overcoming an obstacle, I remind myself that new problems and bigger challenges come with trying new things. Sure, I could keep doing the same things over and over again and continue facing the same hurdles, but I want to forge a new path forward in my life. That's going to mean new trials and challenges.

When we take time to review and analyze the difficult times in our lives, we can learn to appreciate the lessons they teach us. When we step back and ask ourselves, "How did I grow from this" or "What did I learn from this," we can turn almost any situation into a positive one.

Easier said than done, right? If you struggle with positivity, how can you remind yourself to practice positivity, especially if you're busy trying to persevere through a tough time?

Personally, I practice daily journaling. Inside my goal planner, I write down my daily wins. They don't have to be huge wins, but they certainly can be. Some days they're simple, everyday tasks that I completed when I really didn't feel like it. Other days they're big milestones towards achieving my goals. The key is to focus on things you can be proud of even if that thing seems silly or small.

Another thing you can do in your daily planner is to practice gratitude journaling. Write down three to five things you're thankful for every day and be sure to mix it up. As you build a routine around daily journaling, you can begin to explore your thoughts and feelings on paper. I'm often surprised what I learn from my written reflections.

If you're really struggling with positivity or perseverance, you could hang inspirational quotes or messages in your favorite spaces. I've even heard of people setting alarms on their phones for a reminder to recenter throughout the day or to practice purposeful self-affirmations. The strategies can vary from person to person, so be sure to explore what works best for you.

When you embrace the struggle and persevere through difficult situations, you become stronger, and you establish a positive confidence in your ability to weather the ups and downs in your life. This resilience will then allow you to take on even more significant challenges with less effort.

When we choose to view the world through a positive lens and embrace our struggle, we allow ourselves to move forward unencumbered by the extra weight of negativity. We stop fighting against lessons that life is trying to teach us. We learn, we grow, and we become open to new experiences.

4. The Responsibility Mindset

Because Goal Getters work to cultivate a positive mindset, they also understand that they are 100 percent responsible for their lives. This concept is the one that I see the most push back on, and before I unpack it, I have to warn you that this mindset is probably the most controversial one in this chapter. Are you ready?

Develop a Goal Getter's Mindset

Here we go.

As we go through life, things are going to happen that hinders our progress. Some of these things may cause us to stumble for a short time while others may bring us to a complete stand still. We can't control every card life deals our way. We can, however, control how we play the cards we're dealt.

That's why I believe that, as an aspiring Goal Getter, it's important that you take 100 percent responsibility for your life.

> *"How can I be responsible for things that happen to me—things that are beyond my control?"*

This is a question I hear quite a bit, and the short answer is you can't, but you can control how you react to the situations that life throws your way.

Like I said, this one is a hard concept for many people to accept. I myself struggled to adopt this mindset early on in life.

I've been laid off from work twice in my life. The first time, I was newly married, and my wife and I had just bought our first home at the young age of nineteen. I had a pretty bad attitude about getting the axe. I had done everything right. I had followed the rules. I had even jumped through several hoops that many of my coworkers skipped. They kept their jobs. I didn't.

"How can they lay me off," I fumed.

I was furious, and I allowed myself to feel like a victim. I hated that feeling—the feeling of helplessness. I didn't know it then, but what I came to realize later in life is that the feeling of helplessness that I felt didn't come from the company or it's actions; it came from within myself.

I was powerless when it came to keeping that job because I couldn't prevent myself from being laid off, but I didn't have to allow that situation to make me feel helpless. I didn't have to let it ruin my attitude. I may not have been responsible for losing my job, but I was responsible for how I reacted and for the resentment I harbored for my ex-boss.

As it turned out, I wasn't helpless; I just allowed myself to feel that way. I scrambled and found another job waiting tables within a few weeks. I discovered that the only thing holding me back—the only thing keeping me from moving forward—was me.

Flash forward several years and several jobs later. Once again, I was working for a company that ebbed and flowed with fluctuating demand. I had worked hard for a couple of years, but it wasn't my dream job. So when the day came that I got laid off for the second time in my life, I looked for the opportunity in the unfortunate situation.

I had been working at a video production company for free at the same time as the paying job I was about to leave. I was happy to work for free for the experience, but I hoped it would turn into a full-time job eventually, but I was only waiting and hoping. I wasn't taking action towards that goal.

When I received the news of the impending layoff, I thanked my employer for the two weeks notice and immediately talked to my other boss about turning the internship into a paying job. He agreed almost instantly. All I had to do was ask!

No, losing a job isn't fun, and there are far worse things that can happen in life. Sometimes there's nothing you can do to stop bad things from happening, but you can control how you react and how you respond.

Develop a Goal Getter's Mindset

The first time I was laid off, I allowed myself to harbor bad feelings. The second time, however, I knew that I could get another job if I tried hard enough.

In both situations, I was able to hustle and find a new job when life forced my hand. The only difference was the attitude I allowed myself to have during the process.

I hate to say this, but crummy things are going to happen to you in your life at some point. It's far easier said than done, especially in the moment, but try not to dwell on these misfortunes or allow them to hold you back. Instead, take responsibility for your life and your future, chart your own path, and move forward in spite of the difficulty.

Life is unfair to everyone at some point, whether it seems like it or not. Some have it far worse than others. Some people allow misfortune to stop them cold in their tracks. They give up, they lose hope, and they stop trying altogether. Others continue pressing forward towards their goals no matter what. They key difference is the mindset that they choose to live by.

No matter what happens to you in your life, only you can be responsible for how you play the cards you're dealt. No matter what happens, try to maintain a positive attitude and keep pressing forward.

5. The Self-Belief Mindset

When you decide to become 100 percent responsible for your entire life, you accept that anything is possible and that the only thing holding you back is you. Yes, it's true, whatever the mind can conceive and believe, the mind can achieve. Napoleon Hill made that quote famous years ago, and it's still true today.

Sure, some things may be nearly impossible due to obvious

limitations. For example, if you're 4 foot 6 inches tall, you may not have the best shot at getting into the NBA. I'm not saying it would be impossible, but the chances would certainly be slim.

What I am saying, however, is that if you genuinely believe in something, you can achieve it.

Take Kyle Maynard, a man born with a rare condition known as congenital amputation, where fibrous bands prevent the development of fetal limbs. [7] Growing up, he played football. In high school, he wrestled and won thirty-six matches his senior year. [8] He's an author, speaker, and he's best known for becoming the first quadruple amputee to ascend Mount Kilimanjaro without the aid of prosthetics. [9]

How did he do it?

He worked hard and stayed focused. He didn't accept limitations, and he didn't make excuses. Above all, he believed in himself.

We could also look at competitive CrossFitter Ruth Hitchen. In 2017 she was training for a 100-mile bike ride when she was struck by a car, an accident that left her hospitalized with severe injuries including smashed bones, a brain bleed, and several dislocations. [10]

Doctors told Ruth that she was lucky to be alive, and that she would need to find some new, less physical hobbies. She was devastated but determined to prove everyone wrong. With a boot on her leg, sling on her arm, and a careful eye on her blood pressure, she gradually got herself back into her CrossFit gym. She believed that she could get back on top again, and less than two years later, and in spite of a long, slow road to recovery, Ruth won the Fittest in the City London 2019.

That's what Goal Getters do. They believe in themselves.

When you think about your dream life, what do you see? Do you see your true dream, or is it obscured from view by the limitations placed there by yourself or the people around you?

When you think about your dreams, do you honestly believe that they're possible? Do you believe that you can set goals and work towards achieving your dreams? If so, that belief will be the fuel that drives you forward. If not, that disbelief will be the anchor that holds you back.

As you dive deeper and deeper into this book and the workbook, you're going to encounter thoughts and ideas that will challenge you. You're going to come across exercises and guided worksheets that will help you to overcome your fears, self-limiting beliefs, and so much more.

I designed this book to help you work through the things that are holding you back from your dreams, but for it to work, you have to believe that it *can* work.

Maybe you've aimed high and failed before so you're unsure if anything will ever work for you. Or maybe you've never had the self-confidence to shoot for your dreams at all. No matter your story was before today, I'm asking you to dig deep and try to find a way to believe in yourself. I know; it's a big ask, but I believe that each and every person in this world was designed for something great. That greatness may look different for everyone, but I believe it's there inside of you. All you have to do is believe it, too.

Trust me; you've got this!

6. The Act "As if" Mindset

Have you ever heard the old saying, "Fake it until you make it"? While I'm not condoning pretending to be someone you're not, I think a lot can be gained from stepping into the mind of the person you want to become and exploring the possibilities.

Take this, for example: if you wanted to be a high-level executive in a Fortune 500 company, you could act *as if* you've already achieved that goal and then try to imagine what life looks like. Let's look at this a little bit closer.

If you were this high-level, Fortune 500 executive today, how would you act? What would you wear? How would you spend your time and who would you spend your time with?

Asking yourself these types of questions is a great way to get into the headspace of the person you're hoping to become. And, as you begin to explore this potential future version of yourself, you will start to notice new things that you didn't see before. Your perspective will begin to change, and you'll start acting like a Fortune 500 executive.

As you act *as if* and you begin to form your life around this vision for your future, you'll start attracting new people into your life, you'll gain attention and favor at work, and the decisions you make will cause your life to drift closer to your dream.

When you act as if your dream has already come true, your dream will slowly begin to come true. In a way, it's a lot like a self-fulfilling prophecy. By living a life that is congruent with the future you want to have, you build towards your future on purpose.

Remember, you're 100 percent responsible for your life. Whatever future you're dreaming of, act *as if* it were already true, believe it's possible, and start taking actions towards making your dream come true today.

7. The "You Are What You Eat" Mindset

As the saying goes, "You are what you eat." If you eat a steady diet of junk food, your body will become unhealthy. If you eat a regular diet of healthy foods, then hopefully your body would be healthy. Makes sense, right?

Well, the same is true for our minds. We are what we eat.

As you can see in this chapter, being a successful, longterm Goal Getter is significantly easier when you foster a positive, healthy mindset—a mindset that thrives on healthy inputs and influences.

It would be considerably more difficult to believe in our own potential if we *only* interacted with people who were ruled by self-limiting beliefs and learned helplessness. (More on these later.)

It would be difficult to maintain a positive outlook on life if we were to *only* surround ourselves with pessimists and negative thinkers.

It would be nearly impossible to persevere if everyone around us gave up at the first sight of trouble.

While that might make sense on paper, I'm not suggesting you begin cutting people out of your life. I am, however, asking you to be mindful of the people you surround yourself with and make sure to bring balance to your circle.

We all have a friend or family member that tends to lean more towards the eternal pessimist side of things. That's okay! Love them for who they are, but make sure you don't allow their pessimistic world view drown out your own dream for the future. In order to feed your mind a healthy diet, find a few new friends that bring a positive perspective to your life.

You could seek out a mentor, join a mastermind group, or join an online community of like-minded individuals. You could join some local groups or clubs in your community. There are numerous possibilities, but be sure to surround yourself with people who have a positive impact on your life, broaden your perspective, and open your mind up to a whole new world of possibilities.

It's not just the people we hang around, either. It's the TV we watch, the material we read, the podcasts and YouTube channels we subscribe to. If we're not careful about the content we feed our minds, our mindset can become corrupted. Worst of all, it's extremely difficult to know when these negative influences are impacting your mindset.

Take social media, for example. For many, these online communities have become the default way of sharing news, invitations to events, family updates, and so much more, but they're also the highlight reels for most people's lives. For many, this can be difficult to remember, and it can cause people to compare their worst days to other people's best days. Has this happened to you? Maybe it has and you didn't even realize it. Feelings of jealousy, envy, fear of missing out (aka "fomo"), and other similar emotions are difficult to recognize and painful to admit.

Personally, I've logged into Facebook a time or two and saw some local people doing some huge, exciting things and instantly felt like I was behind or that their *thing* was more impactful than my *thing*.

Theodore Roosevelt once said, "Comparison is the thief of joy," and it's true, but it's also difficult to avoid because it takes mindfulness and a strong sense of self-awareness.

When you consume a particular form of content or media, try to pay close attention to how it makes you feel. Do you suddenly feel sad, angry, stressed, envious, demotivated, or discouraged? If so, this could be a sign that you're not feeding your mind in a healthy way.

Longterm exposure to negative influences can greatly impact your mindset and reduce your ability to focus on your goals and dreams. These things are difficult to spot, but take some time and reflect on your influences. How do each of them make you feel? Do they add to your life, or subtract?

I have friends who have completely cut Facebook from their lives for this very reason. That's a huge sacrifice because I'm sure they miss out on invites, family news, and so on, but they're trading those things so that they can protect their mindset.

Again, I'm not suggesting that you start cutting every negative thing from your life, but walking away from some negative things could be one solution. You could also begin balancing those negative influences with more positive inputs.

Social media got you down? Hang a quote or two by your monitor to remind yourself that "Comparison is the thief of joy." Have some family or friends that leave you feeling frustrated or upset? Trade some of that time for time with a new friend or mentor.

The solution could look different for each and every person, but at the end of the day, to stay focused on becoming Better Every Day, be sure to surround yourself with positive influences and feed your mind a healthy diet of positivity and success.

8. The Unlimited Potential Mindset

Can you imagine what life would be like if you were never able to reach your greatest potential? It sounds sad, right? I'm sure we've all known someone who didn't live up to his or her potential, even though we knew they were capable of so much more.

Crush Your Goals!

But what if you never reached your greatest potential, not because you didn't try, but because there was no limit to what you could achieve? What if, day after day, you worked hard, leveled up, and became better, but then found that there was another level to reach?

What would you do? How would you respond to such a situation? Would you get discouraged, or would you excitedly shoot for the next level in your life?

This is an essential aspect of goal setting, because each time you reach a goal that you've set for yourself, you have one of two decisions to make: 1) stay where you are because you're done trying; you're content, or 2) shoot for the next level in your life and see how high you can go.

Which would you choose?

I mentioned this earlier, but several years ago I decided that I wanted to get into the 1,000-pound club at my gym. Because I never attempted this goal before, I had nowhere to go but up. In fact, prior to setting this goal, I had never done a single squat because I heard they could hurt your knees. On top of that, I had never tried deadlifts because I heard that they were a surefire way to damage your back. Those fears aside, I wanted to get into this club.

For the sake of time, I'll skip over the training that ensued over the next year or two and cut to the end.

On Christmas Eve 2015, I achieved my goal. Hooray for me! After that, I kept training and a year later, I found myself lifting my way into the 1,250-pound club. Hooray for me again!

But here's the problem: I accepted the 1,250-pound club as my limit and I quit trying. I didn't think that the next level, the 1,500-pound club, was possible for me, and I ended up wasting the entire next year. I kept lifting, but at best I was maintaining,

either way time is flying by...

not growing or improving. I accepted the 1,250-pou
my maximum potential and stopped pushing myself. But
why?

For some reason, I didn't shoot for that next level. Perhaps it seemed too big. In retrospect, I only had to add 100 pounds to my deadlift and squat and 50 pounds to my bench, neither of which were unreasonable goals. Maybe I lost interest. I'm not entirely sure. Either way, I quit and I decided to stay put, content with my achievement.

In reality, however, when you decide to stay where you are, you're really moving in reverse. This may sound odd, but there is no sitting still in life. You're either moving forward or backward, because as soon as you decide to sit still, life continues to move on by.

I don't say this to be discouraging—quite the opposite. As you dive deeper into this book and into goal setting, you're going to achieve many amazing things. Some will be so great that it will be difficult to believe that you could achieve more. You're also going to hit some plateaus along the way. That's okay—as long as you remind yourself that you're always capable of more.

Sometimes this could look like achieving a new personal record in a goal you've set before, like jumping from the 1,000-pound club to the 1,250-pound club. Other times, your unlimited potential could mean experimenting with something entirely new, like learning a new language that you previously thought would be impossible.

So as you begin to set some big goals for yourself, I want to encourage you to begin to believe in your own unlimited potential. Believe that you can do anything you set your mind to, whether that is pushing your goals higher and higher, or exploring new and exciting goals altogether.

After you've achieved a goal, look for the next level and raise the bar or look for a new goal to set for yourself. As a Goal Getter, there's always another level to reach, and you do have unlimited potential. Accept nothing less for yourself and watch your success grow!

9. The GETMO Mindset

No matter what you're looking to achieve in your life, I think we can all agree that there are countless strategies for achieving success, but which techniques make the biggest impact? The last mindset I want to share with you is a game changer because it can shave months or even years off of your timeline, but it's also one of the trickiest mindsets to master, especially if you struggle with perfectionism like I do.

If you haven't heard this before, or if you have and you're having trouble accepting it, I want to state this last concept very clearly: perfection is impossible.

Your initial reaction might be "duh," but if you take a moment to reflect, you might begin to see how the quest for perfection causes you to procrastinate, put off your goals for *someday*, or cause you to spend years on pursuing a goal that could be achieved in a matter of months. Trust me; I've fallen victim to the perfection/procrastination trap more times that I care to admit, but as you move forward with this book and with your goals, it's important to keep reminding yourself that perfection is impossible.

I originally had the idea for my blog, Daily New Year's, back in October of 2017, and I worked hard on it for months. Eight long months later, and I still hadn't launched my site to share my ideas with the world. Why? In my mind, it just wasn't *done* yet.

Or at least that's what I kept telling myself.

Develop a Goal Getter's Mindset

"Just go home and take it live," one of my coworkers nudged.

"It's just not quite done yet," I argued.

"It's a blog—it can never be done. Just launch what you have," she insisted.

"Okay, I'll go home and get as much done as I can tonight and I will launch first thing in the morning," I assured her.

I work at a website development company. We convince our clients to launch when they're "not 100 percent *done*" all the time because it's better to launch and start collecting feedback as early as possible than it is to leave a site sitting on a hidden server for months on end. And 100 percent done is never possible. As soon as you go live, there's something to add, change, or update.

But for some reason, I couldn't take my own advice without a little push from a friend. (Thanks, Katie!)

It happens to all of us: we convince ourselves that the timing is wrong or that whatever we're working on isn't *done* yet. It's a way to keep ourselves from finishing what we've started—to keep ourselves distracted and busy. But this mindset keeps us from moving on from one goal so that we may pursue the next.

For a long time, I struggled to complete this book. Instead of starting with a rough draft manuscript and getting an editor involved, I was trying to write, design, and edit the book all at the same time, chapter by chapter. It was a mess and I was going nowhere fast! I was spinning my wheels because I wanted to get it as close to perfect as I could before sharing it with another human being, my editor.

Then I read this quote from one of my favorite authors, Jon Acuff, "90 percent perfect and shared with the world always changes more lives than 100 percent perfect and stuck in your head." It was a game-changer!

I immediately enrolled in an online course, stripped the book down to the basics, and set a goal to get a completed rough draft done and to my editor. The quest for perfection was holding me back, as it so often does, but I finally broke free.

The need for perfection is one of my greatest struggles as a Goal Getter, but knowing that about myself helps me work around it. I have a group of mentors, and I'm in a Mastermind group with several high-achieving men from my community. They all help me to move past my perfection problem by encouraging me to share what I have so far or by reminding me of a message I learned at the 2019 Global Leadership Summit.

Co-Founder and Senior Paster at Life.Church, Craig Groeschel opened the summit with a passionate and inspiring talk about a concept he calls GETMO, or "Good Enough to Move On." Just like Jon's quote above, this was a massive game changer in my life. In his talk, he reminded the audience that perfection is often the thief of progress, and the quest for perfection will limit what we're able to achieve in life.

As you move forward with this book and begin to explore the goals you want to set for you life, remember, progress over perfection always wins the day.

You're going to dream up some big things for your life. Maybe you want to start a new business or non-profit or perhaps you want to master a new skill such as cooking or writing poetry. No matter which goals you decide to pursue in the days, weeks, months, and years ahead, try to remember that nothing is going to be perfect, especially at first. In fact, as you struggle through starting something new, what you produce might be pretty imperfect at first (maybe even bad), but the only way to improve is to keep trying.

If you want to start a business or a non-profit, remember that a business that isn't open isn't making money and a non-profit that isn't open isn't helping people. I'm not suggesting that you rush into something without thinking it through, but your new business or non-profit won't be perfect on day one, and you won't have everything figured out (not even close!), but at some point, what you have will have to be good enough to move on.

If you want to become a master chef, cooking for people and requesting honest feedback are going to be super important. Take classes, practice at home, but at some point, share your progress with friends and family or enter into some competitions. If you want to become a published poet, write often and share your work with other writers, professors, or poetry fans. Not everyone will enjoy or appreciate your work, but don't wait for it to be perfect before you decide to share it with the world.

As you dive deeper into the book ahead, I'm sure you'll find that it's far from perfect. I'm sure I've missed a grammatical thing or two or could have included some additional strategies, quotes, inspiring stories, and so on, but at the end of the day, I wanted to release a book that would help people just like you to crush their goals.

If it weren't for my friends and family and people like Jon Acuff and Craig Greoschel, I would still be writing, editing, and rewriting. My innate need for things to be perfect is something I struggle against everyday, but I'm always trying (with help) to improve upon my mindset and overcome my hangups. It can be frustrating, but the last thing I'll tell you here is that nothing can be perfect, especially our mindsets. There will always be room for growth and improvement, but we can't let that keep us from progressing.

It's Not About Mastering the Mindset

Having a Goal Getter's mindset doesn't mean you've mastered all the *right* mentalities while avoiding all the *wrong* ones; it means that you know which mindsets will serve you best and you strive to live them. But we all have blind spots.

As you've just seen, I struggle with perfectionism, but I've learned this about myself, and I've built a support group around myself to combat this very problem. It's okay to struggle with the concepts in the chapter. If you haven't mastered all of these mindsets, don't worry! If you had all of this stuff mastered already, you probably don't need this book!"

As you begin walking your own personal development journey, you're going to learn countless new things about yourself, and that's a good thing, but it's also a hard thing. As you go through life, it's important to look within yourself, to learn about yourself, and to grow into the person you want to become, but the process will also begin to reveal flaws you didn't know you had. I know it has for me! Over the past few years I've learned a lot about myself, and it wasn't always easy to acknowledge my flaws, but I'm grateful for my journey and the growth I've gained from it so far.

For example, I didn't always believe in the Better Every Day mindset. Because I've had my struggles with perfectionism, I used to think something was either 100 percent perfect and finished or not done at all. As you can imagine, this prevented me from getting a lot of stuff done. If you struggle with perfectionism, you know how draining it is to never feel like your work is good enough. Then, because nothing is ever good enough, you never complete anything and that makes you feel bad, too.

Fortunately, I learned how to overcome this problem through

a shift in my mindset, but perfectionism isn't the only thing I've overcome. I've struggled with self doubt in many areas of my life, and I certainly didn't believe in unlimited potential or that I was completely responsible for my life.

Over time, though, through personal development and self reflection, I began to change my mindset. As I adopted the concepts in this chapter, I started to see major changes in my life. In high school I had an extremely difficult time in English and thought I would never be able to be a writer. In fact, I was so bad in English class that I told myself I hated writing, so becoming an author wasn't even on my radar. I was blind to that option because of how awful I thought I was at writing.

Now, because I have a message and the passion to share it, writing has become one of my favorite things to do, in spite of my skill level. I can't tell you how many times I've turned my back on or closed my eyes to the possibilities around me because I hadn't adopted these mindsets.

But here's the deal, it's really hard to look in the mirror and ask, "How can I be better? What's important to me? Do I take 100 percent responsibility for my life? What am I capable of? Am I the person holding me back?" That's what personal development does; it pushes you to reflect, to grow, and to evolve, mindset and all.

So many of us walk through life with our eyes closed. I know I was for a very long time. We're comfortable, content, and we're happy just going through the motions—until we aren't.

It's on the day that we realize we're not happy with where we're at that we open our eyes and start working towards self improvement and sharpening our mindset. But, opening your eyes and seeing all the ways you could be better can be overwhelming. True, but it's also a great thing because it's at this point when the best growth begins to happen and you start becoming Better Every Day.

If you don't feel like you have the *perfect* Goal Getter's mindset right now, that's okay. Keep going. Complete the exercises in the corresponding workbook and record your thoughts. Try to get to know yourself a little bit better. Then dive deeper into this book. As you start identifying and setting goals for yourself and begin working hard to crush them, the mindset will begin to come along with it. If you need to, refer back to this chapter when you need a refresher.

This book wasn't written as a one-and-done read through. It's meant to serve and guide your goal-setting journey for years to come, so don't hesitate to revisit the chapters from time to time. Doing so will be a fantastic reminder for just how far you've come since the last time you explored these pages.

Develop a Goal Getter's Mindset

CHAPTER RECAP

Key Takeaways

- **Focusing on your mindset** is the foundation on which to begin building your goal-setting success.
- **Having a Goal Getter's mindset** doesn't mean you've mastered all the *right* mentalities while avoiding all the *wrong* ones; it means that you know which mindsets will serve you best and you strive to live them.
- **We all have blind spots.** Don't let that discourage you. Personal Development is about discovering your blind spots and working to improve them.

The Nine Goal Getter Mindsets:

- **1. The Better Every Day Mindset**
  Better Every Day mindset means that as long as you're trying, you're getting better, and as long as you're getting better, you're winning.

- **2. The Lifelong Learner Mindset**
  Goals are all about growth. And if goals are all about growth, then a life rich in learning is critical to the process.

- **3. The Positivity and Perseverance Mindset**
  Goal setting is not all sunshine and rainbows, so we have to generate positivity within ourselves and persevere through the ups and downs.

- **4. The Responsibility Mindset**
  We can't control every card life deals our way, but we can control how we play the cards we're dealt. It's important that you take 100 percent responsibility for your life.

- **5. The Self Belief Mindset**

Whatever the mind can conceive and believe, the mind can achieve. Self belief will be the fuel that drives you forward. Lack of Self belief will be the anchor that holds you back.

- **6. The Act As if Mindset**
When you act as if your dream has already come true by living a life that is congruent with the future you want to have, you build towards your dream life on purpose.

- **7. The You Are What You Eat Mindset**
To stay focused on becoming Better Every Day, surround yourself with positive influences and feed your mind a healthy diet of success.

- **8. The Unlimited Potential Mindset**
Unlimited Potential means that you never accept the limitations placed upon you and you constantly shoot for the next level in your life.

- **9. The GETMO Mindset**
Perfection is impossible and striving for it only causes procrastination. Embrace that sometimes things are Good Enough to Move on. Progress over perfection always wins the day.

Memorable Quotes

☆ *"Goals aren't about being perfect; they're about being better than you were before."* —Elyse Lyons

☆ *"90 percent perfect and shared with the world always changes more lives than 100 percent perfect and stuck in your head."* —Jon Acuff

Put it into Practice

↪ Complete the corresponding self-assessments to begin enhancing your Goal Getter's mindset.

Rapid Recap: Section 1

In this section of the book, we've learned about connecting a strong *why* with our goals. Having a strong *why* is the solid foundation on which to build our goals. Without it, our goals stand little chance of success.

Why provides clarity for which goals are our true goals and helps to avoid the motivation trap. When we start with a strong *why*, our motivations for achieving a goal are intrinsic and our desire to achieve the goal overpowers even the most difficult or tiring day.

In this section, I also shined a light on the six biggest fears that keep people from setting goals: the fear of loss, the fear of judgment and rejection, the fear of discontent, the fear of the unknown, the fear of failure, and the fear of success.

These six fears do not discriminate. Whether we know it or not, at least one of these fears is present in our lives, and often, there is more than one. The good news is that we can learn to recognize and manage our fears, but only if we acknowledge their presence in our lives.

Remember, courage isn't the absence of fear, but the ability to move forward in spite of it.

We also learned how to establish and strengthen our self-confidence so that we can move forward with certainty and self-assurance. When it comes to goal setting, self-confidence occurs when you set a goal and know right from the start that you've got a great chance of crushing it. It takes time to build, but self-discipline is one of the best ways to boost your confidence.

Lastly, we took a look at which philosophies and mindsets will serve us best on our longterm, goal-setting journey. From seeking to become Better Every Day to avoiding the procrastinating perfectionist trap, we learned nine different belief systems that Goal Getters tend to live by.

More importantly, we learned that the aim isn't to master the mindsets. It's not about perfecting all nine concepts; it's about understanding them and striving to live them as best we can. We all have blindspots, but as we continue to grow, we can work towards shining a light on those areas of our lives so that we can make the improvements needed to reach our goals.

In the next section, we're going to begin to dive into goal-setting techniques and strategies. First, we're going to learn about a new goal-setting framework. Goodbye SMART Goals—say hello to **The FOCUSED Framework**.

After that, I'm going to share four universal goals that you should start setting as soon as you feel ready. This chapter and its worksheets may take some time because I'm going to ask you to begin charting your goals as we go along. Don't worry; it's going to be a blast!

Rapid Recap

One of the biggest things that holds Goal Getters back is their inability to properly prioritize their goals and their time. In chapter seven, I'm going to arm you with five proven prioritization strategies that will give you the clarity and freedom to focus on what matters most.

Finally, we're going to talk about the best tools for tracking your success. From journals to apps and everything in between, I'm going to show you the best ways to track and crush your goals.

So if you're ready, let's do this!

SECTION 2
GETTING STARTED WITH GOAL SETTING

The FOCUSED Framework™

"If you want to be happy, set a goal that commands your thoughts, liberates your energy and inspires your hopes."

– Andrew Carnegie

How many goal-setting frameworks, strategies, and techniques have you tried in the past?

Me? I had been using the SMART Goals [1] method for years, but truthfully, I didn't always see the success I wanted. Sure, my goals were specific, measurable, yadda yadda yadda, but I found that my success was still hit or miss. Why?

Personally, I think it's because the SMART Goals method lacks an emotional connection to the goal you're trying to achieve.

Don't you want to set goals that are exciting? Wouldn't it be nice if a goal was challenging, yet energizing? Wouldn't it be

---

[1] SMART Goals are Specific, Measurable, Achievable, Relevant and Time-bound.

great if you felt drawn to a goal, rather than obligated to stick with it?

That's what I was missing: an emotional connection.

So I decided to create a new framework—a new criteria by which to evaluate our goals, one built around emotion, energy, and excitement.

Success in goal setting stems from identifying goals that give you a strong sense of passion and purpose, and if you follow this framework, that's exactly what you're going to find. Before we dive into specific goal-setting strategies, I want to outline this new framework, letter by letter.

The FOCUSED Framework

FOCUSED is an acronym that stands for Future Focused, Optimistic, Challenging, Unforgettable, Significant, Energizing, and Deadline Driven.

Each of the letters has a corresponding question that will help guide you towards setting goals that truly matter to you, goals that add value to your life, and that you get pumped up.

If you're ready, let's dive in!

Future Focused

I believe all good goals should contribute to a brighter future and give us something remarkable to look forward to. Maybe that's a healthier life, financial independence, a fulfilling career, or something else entirely.

Whatever it is, try thinking about where you want to be in one, five, or even ten years from now. Can you imagine where you'll be in ten years or what your life will look like? Don't panic; I know this is difficult and maybe even a little scary, but nothing is concrete. For now, we're just dreaming.

We touched on Blue-Sky Thinking a little bit already, and we'll dive deeper into that topic in chapter six. For now, try to imagine your future and just know that your goals should be designed to help you see that future come true.

With each of your goals in mind, ask yourself:

> *"Is this goal going to move me forward and contribute to the future that I envision for myself?"*

If the answer is yes, you're on the right track!

Here's a Personal Example:

Someday, I want to be a professional speaker who travels the world and shares the Daily New Year's message. In the next five to ten years, I would love to have the opportunity to speak on a stage to a crowd of about ten thousand people, similar to the Global Leadership Summit, if not that event specifically.

This goal is something that is set in the future, five to ten years from now, but not all of your goals have to be set that far in the future. They could be weekly, monthly, quarterly, or annual goals. The idea is that your goals all lead to the dream life you want for yourself in the future. I want to be a professional speaker and this goal will help get me there.

⊘ My goal is future-focused.

Okay, once you come up with goals that are future-focused, it's time to see how they fit into the rest of the framework.

Optimistic

Optimism is critical for goal setting. Who would want to work on goals that are hopelessly unattainable? Who would want to work towards a goal that's not exciting?

Sure, goals should be challenging (we're getting there), but they should also be fun! Goals shouldn't always be a chore—they should bring joy to your life, ignite your passion, and help make your dreams come true.

Wouldn't you agree?

With each of your goals in mind, ask yourself:

> *"Is this goal an optimistic one that will make a positive impact on my life, and am I optimistic that I can achieve it?"*

It's important to note the two sides of this: you should be optimistic about the goal AND your ability to achieve it.

Back to my example:

Becoming a professional speaker and addressing an audience of ten thousand people would help me spread the Daily New Year's message, open me up to a broader audience, and would bring me tremendous joy.

Additionally, I've been seeking more opportunities to speak in public, and I'm getting better each time. I'm optimistic that, with training, practice, and time, I could achieve this goal.

- ✓ My goal is optimistic.

Now, didn't I mention that goals should be optimistic, yet challenging?

Challenging

The "A" in SMART goals stands for *attainable*, but if goals are too easy to reach, then there tends to be less pride in reaching them.

I believe goals should stretch you. If every goal you set is easily attainable, then perhaps you're not shooting high enough. On the flip side, goals that are too difficult to reach are discouraging. "Too easy" and "too difficult" will vary from person to person. For example, if you're not a routine runner, aiming to win the Boston Marathon would probably be too difficult. However, aiming to complete a 5k may be too easy given most people can walk a 5k in forty-five minutes or so. Aiming to complete your first half-marathon in under three hours might a good goal.

Again, this will vary from person to person, but keep in mind that growth happens at the edge of your comfort zone, and that's why I recommend that your goals be challenging. It may take some trial and error, but don't get discouraged.

With each of your goals in mind, ask yourself:

> *"Is this goal going to require me to stretch and grow? Will it be difficult to achieve? Am I going to have to push myself?"*

Back to my example:

Landing a speaking gig at the Global Leadership Summit or an equivalent will be no easy task. Each year, top-tier speakers in the leadership development field are carefully selected to come and speak to the worldwide audience.

Over the next five to ten years, I'm going to have to practice, book countless engagements, and become an authority on goal setting, but I believe I have the discipline to see this goal through if I work hard enough.

- ✓ My goal is Challenging.

Be sure not to set goals that are so difficult that you don't have any hope in achieving them. The aim is to stretch yourself and grow beyond the person you are today, not to achieve perfection overnight.

Unforgettable

It's always a great idea to write your goals down and refer to them regularly. After all, people who write their goals down are 42 percent more likely to achieve them. [11]

However, I've found that unforgettable goals are the ones I enjoy chasing the most. Whether I write them down or not, unforgettable goals are the goals that I wake up every day ready to work towards.

This book, my blog, the podcast—these are all things that I feel excited to work on every day. They're completely unforgettable!

When trying to pick goals that you're going to succeed in crushing, make sure they're the ones you can't seem to forget. Is there something in your mind that you've wanted to do for years, but haven't? That's what I'm talking about. Unforgettable goals are the ones that seem to be embedded in your mind.

With each of your goals in mind, ask yourself:

> "Am I so passionate about achieving this goal that it's all I can think about? Do I wake up each and every day excited to work towards it?"

Back to my example:

While I'm not ready to start taking on speaking engagements today, it is something that continues to make my list of goals. (In a later chapter we'll discuss how to prioritize your goals and to avoid goal competition.)

Today, this book, my blog, and the podcast are my top goals. Next, I want to layer in a YouTube channel. After that, maybe I'll be ready to start speaking to live groups of aspiring Goal Getters.

Until then, though, my goal of speaking to a massive audience is not one that I forget about. It's always there on my list of long-term goals. It's always in the forefront of my mind.

- ✓ My goal is Unforgettable.

Which goals do you keep thinking about over and over? Those goals are a good place to start when thinking about what you hope to achieve in the coming years.

Significant

Significance can have a few meanings. Goals that have a huge impact on your life are significant. Goals that are important to you right now are significant. Goals that are going to take your life to a new level are significant.

Why would we waste time chasing goals of little or no significance? It happens all the time: we set goals that mean very little to us on a personal level, and therefore, we have little motivation or desire to achieve them.

Are your goals significant to you?

With each of your goals in mind, ask yourself:

> *"Is this goal significant to me and my current place in life? Does it add significance to my life? Is this goal going to take me to a new level?"*

Back to my example:

Speaking to an audience of ten thousand people about goal setting, Daily New Year's, and the Better Every Day mindset would be extremely significant to me. It would give me a new platform for sharing my message, allow me to build credibility, and it would help me realize my dream of becoming a professional speaker.

- ✓ My goal is Significant.

It's important to note that goals that aren't significant to you today may be significant later in life. Every season of life comes with new goals, priorities, and ambitions. If a goal is unforgettable, but it's not significant to you right now, understand that it's okay to shelve that goal and revisit it later in life.

The timing may not be right today, but when you revisit the goal later in life when the timing is right, the goal will give you an abundance of passion and energy.

Energizing

Do your goals get you excited? Do they give you energy? Those are questions that so many people forget to ask when they set goals for themselves. That's why energy is an extremely important part of my framework.

Not all goals are going to give you energy. Between managing deadlines at work or getting all of your housework done this weekend, some goals are just necessary to keep life moving. We don't pick these goals—they seem to pick us.

However, the goals that you set for yourself—those things that you really *want* to do—those goals should give you enormous amounts of energy. Those are the goals that seem to recharge you even as you're working on them.

With each of your goals in mind, ask yourself:

> *"Does this goal get me pumped up and energized? Am I excited to pursue it? Does this goal lift my spirit and attitude?"*

Back to my example:

I find the idea of becoming a professional speaker extremely energizing. Sure, it will be hard work, and it will require me to overcome some fears, but the goal itself will provide its own energy and seeing ten thousand people in the audience will be thrilling, to say the least.

⊘ My goal is Energizing.

Goals that give us energy are the goals that we tend to achieve. Goals that drain our energy and willpower are the goals we tend to abandon. Always try to choose the former.

Deadline Driven

When we're on the receiving end of deadlines, they can be a drag, especially if they're tied to tasks we don't want to do in the first place. But when we use deadlines to achieve our goals, they can provide a motivating sense of urgency.

Shark Tank's Robert Herjavec once said, "A goal without a timeline is just a dream," and he's 100 percent correct. Without a deadline, we're just floating through life looking forward to *someday*. [12]

Assuming our goals are already Future-Focused, Optimistic,

Challenging, Unforgettable, Significant, and Energizing, why wouldn't we want a deadline? Wouldn't we want to see that goal realized sooner rather than later?

With each of your goals in mind, ask yourself:

> *"Does my goal have a finite deadline or a milestone that I can reach?"*

Back to my example:

In the next five to ten years, I would love to have the opportunity to speak on a stage to a crowd of about ten thousand people.

- ⊗ My goal is not Deadline Driven.

Yes, I have a loose timeline for my goal, but not a finite date. As of today, I'm not ready to start my speaking career. I know that I have so much more to learn before I'll be able to put forth my best performance, so I haven't set this goal for myself—yet.

However, I do have it recorded in my goal journal for a later date, and as soon as I'm ready to start taking on speaking engagements, I'm going to revisit this goal and set a finite deadline for myself.

So there it is—**The FOCUSED Framework**. As I mentioned earlier in this chapter, I had been setting goals using the SMART Goals method for years, but my success was far too unpredictable and, for the longest time, I couldn't figure out why.

One day I realized that goal setting shouldn't be a dull, meaningless method for getting more stuff done.

- ⊘ Goal setting should be about self-improvement.

- ✓ Goal setting should be exciting.
- ✓ Goal setting should help us live happy and fulfilling lives.

That's why I came up with **The FOCUSED Framework**. I wanted to set more goals that would help me grow, excite me, and lead to a fulfilling life.

And that's what I want for you, too. If you're ready to get started using **The FOCUSED Framework** to identify and set your goals, simply turn to the next page to get started on the exercises.

But before you do—Keep in mind that your goals don't have to hit all seven items on **The FOCUSED Framework** checklist.

Obviously, the more items you can check off, the better chance you have in seeing success with your goals, but falling one item short does not necessarily mean you shouldn't pursue the goal.

The FOCUSED Framework is not meant to be a black or white or a yes or no approach to identifying goals—it's meant to help you identify which of your goals are strong and which goals may need deeper thought or reflection. Ultimately, which goals you pursue is entirely up to you.

In the next chapter, I'm going to highlight a few different types of goals that I believe everyone should be setting for themselves. With that in mind, feel free to go ahead and use the **The FOCUSED Framework** worksheets in the workbook to begin assessing the goals you have in mind.

However, if you would rather proceed to the next chapter to learn about the four different types of goals you can set, please do so. You can always revisit **The FOCUSED Framework** worksheets later.

CHAPTER RECAP

Key Takeaways

- **SMART Goals** are Specific, Measurable, Achievable, Relevant, and Time-bound, but they lack an emotional connection to the goal itself.
- **Goal setting shouldn't be a dull**, meaningless method for getting more stuff done. Goal setting should be about self-improvement. It should be exciting and help us live happy and fulfilling lives.
- Your goals don't have to hit all seven items on **The FOCUSED Framework** checklist. The more items you can check off, the better chance you have in seeing success with your goals, but falling one or two items short does not necessarily mean you shouldn't pursue the goal.
- **The FOCUSED Framework** is designed to help you evaluate your goals, not to restrict your goals. Use your best judgment and set goals that you're excited to pursue.

The FOCUSED Framework stands for:

- **Future-Focused**
  Good goals should contribute to a brighter future and give us something remarkable to look forward too.
- **Optimistic**
  Who would want to work on goals that are hopelessly unattainable or uninspiring? Choose goals that you're optimistic about pursuing and that you believe you can achieve.
- **Challenging**
  Growth happens at the edge of your comfort zone. Challenging goals will stretch you, take you to new

levels in your life, and keep you energized in the process.

- ⊘ **Unforgettable**
Unforgettable goals are the goals that you wake up every day excited to work towards.
- ⊘ **Significant**
Significant goals have a huge impact on your life and they're important right now.
- ⊘ **Energizing**
The goals that you set for yourself—the things that you really want to achieve—those goals should give your enormous amounts of energy.
- ⊘ **Deadline-Driven**
Assuming our goals are all of the above, why wouldn't you want a deadline?

Memorable Quotes

☆ *"Goals should bring joy to your life, ignite your passion, and help make your dreams come true."*

☆ *"A goal without a timeline is just a dream."*
—Robert Herjavec

Put it into Practice

↪ Use the corresponding worksheets to evaluate each one of your goals using **The FOCUSED Framework**.

↪ If you don't currently have goals that need to be evaluated, skip ahead to the next chapter to learn about four types of goals you can set and circle back to these worksheets later.

Four Universal Goals to Start Setting Today

"Most people overestimate what they can do in one year and underestimate what they can do in ten years."

– Bill Gates

People can usually tell that I'm obsessed with goals, so they often ask me, "What goals do you think I should set?"

I think most people are asking what their specific goals should be, like "Should I be investing in a Roth IRA" or "Should I be taking an online course to improve on a key skill," but those are complicated questions to answer without going deep with each person.

Getting to know every person who reads this book probably isn't possible, at least within the confines of these pages, but if I were to attempt to answer either of the questions above, I would start by asking several more questions first.

For example, at what age do you want to retire? What kind of lifestyle do you want to have in retirement? How much money will it take to live that lifestyle? How much debt do you currently have? When would you need to start saving and how much money would you need to put aside each month to reach your goal? What other investments are you pursuing, if any?

As you can see, helping people identify specific goals takes one-on-one coaching, and going that deep with everyone isn't something we can do here in this book. So instead of going deep with you about your specific goals, I want to teach you about some of the different types of goals that you can set for the different areas of your life.

There are countless types of goals out there, from SMART BHAGs [1] to 25-Year Visions, but my objective isn't to list out a bunch of different types of goals or concepts just for the sake of doing so.

Instead, I want to tell you about the four universal types of goals that changed my life forever.

That may seem crazy, but these goals helped me achieve more than I ever thought possible in less time than I could have imagined. They've helped me stay focused, driven, and excited to pursue my dreams.

These goals worked wonders for me, and I'm confident that they can work wonders for you, too.

1. Long-Term Goals (3-5 Years+)

As a teen and young adult, long-term life goals were a crazy idea to me. You see, I didn't like the education process. I didn't

---

[1] BHAG stands for Big Hairy Audacious Goal, an idea conceptualized in the book, "Built to Last: Successful Habits of Visionary Companies" by James Collins and Jerry Porras. According to Collins and Porras, a BHAG is a long-term goal that changes the very nature of a business' existence.

Four Universal Goals to Start Setting Today

enjoy sitting in class, learning what someone else deemed necessary for my future. High school was awful, and college wasn't much better. They both seemed to drag on forever!

When months felt like years, how was a guy supposed to think five years ahead? All I wanted to do was get school over with so that I could start working and making money.

I'm sure you can relate, right? Maybe you're having trouble focusing on your future goals because of things happening in your life at this very moment.

Maybe you think it will be easier to focus on your future once you move past this phase of your life. Perhaps you're going through a bad breakup, a painful divorce, or you're desperately looking for a new job that you won't hate as much as the one you're working at right now.

Heck, maybe you're in the never-ending cycle of schooling yourself, and it's difficult to see past the years you have left. Trust me, there are always a thousand reasons to not look ahead at your future. But as never-ending as the education process had seemed, I wish I had taken a step back to plan my future better.

As it turns out, four years of college is a blip on the radar. When you graduate, you have to know what comes next; otherwise, you'll end up with a graphic design degree that you rarely use and wish you had an M.B.A. instead. [2]

We can apply the same logic to any season in our lives. We need to take some time to look ahead for what comes next in our lives, or we may not enjoy what we find later.

Lord willing, we'll all get a solid ninety-plus years on this Earth

---

[2] I pursued a graphic design degree because it was fun in high school, and I picked Photoshop up quickly, but I never stopped to think about graphic design as a career. Whoops!

and taking it day-by-day is no way to get where you want to go. That's like taking a road trip without a destination or route in mind. How can you get where you want to go by jumping in the car and driving aimlessly a little bit each day? You can't!

Instead, we all need to be looking ahead five years or so. We need to be looking to the future so that we can better plan our days. One great way to plan your future, whether that is five years or twenty-five years, is to practice Blue-Sky Thinking. I reference this practice several times throughout the book, but I want to dive deeper into this concept here.

Blue-Sky Thinking

I first learned about Blue-Sky Thinking in Brian Tracy's book *GOALS!*, and he touched on an exciting discovery made by Dr. Charles Garfield.

Garfield studied peak performers for more than twenty years, and he specifically analyzed men and women who had only achieved average results for many years but then suddenly achieved massive success in a very short amount of time.

When I read about this discovery, I couldn't help but imagine a line graph. Across the bottom I saw the number of years in a person's life and up the left-hand side was a success score, ranging from zero to one hundred.

If you're picturing this make-believe graph as I did, imagine that there is a line running across a couple decades worth of years that is nearly flat and barely climbing. Then, suddenly, it spikes from an average number like fifty, to a high number like ninety five. What could have caused such a sudden jump in success for these people?

When Garfield sought the answer, he found that all of these individuals had begun using Blue-Sky Thinking.

Four Universal Goals to Start Setting Today

Blue-Sky Thinking is the practice of looking forward into your future and imagining that all things are possible for you, that you have no limits to speak of, and that your life is perfect in every way. That's hard to imagine, or at least I know it was for me!

Maybe your dream life includes a loving spouse, a high-paying career, a beautiful home, and an expensive sports car in the garage. Perhaps in your dream life, you're a real estate tycoon who's worth billions of dollars or you're the founder of a world-changing nonprofit. It really doesn't matter what you imagine as long as you dream big. The sky's the limit!

The idea behind Blue-Sky Thinking is that no dream is unreal or unattainable. For Blue-Sky Thinking to work, you need to remove all limits, including learned helplessness, self-limiting beliefs, and limits that have been placed on you by other people. That may sound simple in theory but can prove challenging in practice.

You see, most people grow up learning what "normal" is supposed to look like, so they often accept what's possible based on someone else's definition of "normal." I'm here to tell you that only you can determine what's possible for you.

So as you think through your dream life remember, this exercise is not grounded in your current reality, so there's no need to make compromises or to settle for small goals. You should be thinking of ridiculous, outlandish, and seemingly impossible things for yourself. Just because you can't afford a million-dollar home today doesn't mean it's off limits in the future.

If it helps to break it down, think through the different aspects of your life, including your professional career, finances, family, health, and even your social life. What does each of these look like in your dream life?

Coming Back to Reality

Once you get into the exercise and you've managed to visualize your dream life, it's time to come back to reality and think about what you would have to do going forward to make this dream a reality. Do not let doubt or fear creep in and kill your dream. Never underestimate your potential. Instead, break things down and analyze them, like so:

- Are you on the right career path or do you need to switch industries to get closer to your dream job?
- What kind of mindset does future you have? Are you hanging around people with that kind of mindset today?
- What does your future spouse or partner look like? How does he or she behave? Where can you go to meet someone like that?

I could go on and on, but I think you get the idea here. Nothing in life is impossible, even though it may seem impossible when you're looking to jump from A to Z.

The concept behind Blue-Sky Thinking is not to trick your mind into jumping from A to Z overnight; the idea is to remove all of the limits in your mind so that you can truly see what's possible in life.

Then you can take a step back and plan the steps to get there, going from A to B, and then on to C and D, and so on. Like I said earlier, when setting long-term goals, it's important to begin with the end in mind. Blue-Sky Thinking gives us a long-term dream life to aim for.

As I've grown a little older, and maybe a little wiser, I've started to realize what my grandparents always said is true: "The older you get, the faster time flies." As time races by, it's important to pause, look ahead, and take stock of where you want your life to go. If you don't, you may not like where you end up.

That's where long-term goal-planning comes into play.

Planning Your Five-Year Future

From what I've seen, there are a few different types of people: those who have no idea what they want their future to be like or how to get it, those who know exactly what they want and how to get it, and about a dozen different degrees of those people in between.

For those of you who have no idea where you want your life to go (and assuming Blue-Sky Thinking didn't work), let's try a couple of other exercises. First, try thinking back over your life and jot down the answers to these questions—feel free to use the note pages at the end of the chapter.

- What are some of your most significant accomplishments in life so far? (As a note, I use the word accomplishments loosely. It doesn't have to be something huge, like being the valedictorian or winning a national competition of some kind. It could be a poem you wrote, a class you did very well in, or even a project you made in shop class.)
- Of your accomplishments, which ones made you most proud and excited? Which ones could you not wait to share with the people in your life?
- Could you expand on those accomplishments and take them further? Could you build on them? If so, how? If you enjoyed woodworking in high school, perhaps you could start making crafts to sell on the side, maybe even open a furniture

rehab store. If you enjoyed writing a poem, maybe you could write an entire book of poems.

These questions should help you identify what gets you excited in life, but if you have trouble thinking back on old accomplishments as a way to plan your future, try this one instead:

✓ What does my life look like in three to five years?

Aside from the obvious answers such as "make more money," what does life look like in five years? Where do you work? Who do you surround yourself with most? Have you started a family? Where do you live? Are you happy?

Don't focus on what you want to accomplish over the next five years. Instead, take five minutes to free write a description of your future five years from now. Don't focus on the *how*, or the tiny details involved; just focus on the future.

This is a little bit like Blue-Sky Thinking, but on a smaller scale. Instead of projecting twenty five years or more into the future, just focus on the next five years.

Here's my five-year vision:

> *"In five years, I would like to have built a community around Daily New Year's that includes hundreds of thousands of people worldwide with more people joining every day.*
>
> *I still work full time, but my wife and I often enjoy the freedom to travel around the world promoting my book and the Daily New Year's message at various events and speaking engagements.*
>
> *My schedule keeps me busy, but I'm healthier than I've ever been. Even while traveling, I continue to focus on my fitness and healthy*

Four Universal Goals to Start Setting Today

> *eating habits.*
>
> *Due to new streams of income, proper financial planning, and a growing business, Callie no longer has to work a regular job and is free to pursue her passions in life.* [3]

Sounds pretty ambitious, right? Attainable or not, that is my vision for my life five years from now.

To get there, I can break it down into a five-year plan that includes things like starting the blog, a YouTube Channel, and a podcast; promoting those channels on social media; growing my audience and email list; improving my public speaking skills; expanding my network; publishing the book; and so on.

Of the four types of goals, long-term goals may seem daunting, maybe even a little scary, but they shouldn't. They should be inspiring!

Remember, goals aren't concrete. Things change, and so can your goals. Setting a five-year goal for yourself today doesn't mean you can't change your mind later, so don't get stuck on the what-ifs that might be running through your mind. It's okay if they evolve and change later on down the road.

Think about your dream life three to five years from now and set some long-term goals that will keep you excited. Have fun with the process and dream big! If you dream so big that you can't fit your vision into five years, make it ten years. Feeling ambitious? Jot down some twenty-year goals.

---

3 Now, I want to mention that my wife is an extraordinarily hard worker. It's not that she doesn't want to work, or can't take care of herself, but I love working and I want to provide enough income through my passions that she can do whatever she wants to in life.

The important thing is, once you have your long-term goals, you can break them down into annual and quarterly goals, starting with a list of goals for the year ahead.

2. Annual and Quarterly Goals

Before we dive into annual and quarterly goals, I have to make a couple of things clear. First, annual goals are not resolutions. Resolutions are those pesky things that we set on December 31st after we've had one too many cocktails.

In a sudden surge of misplaced motivation, we say things like, "I'm going to lose fifty pounds this year" or "I'm going to get serious about fitness and complete an Ironman by June."

I don't know about you, but I've ditched more aspirational resolutions than I can count. They're born of good intentions, but seldom pan out in the end. Annual goals are different though—they're a strategic set of goals that help us get closer to our long-term goals—more on that in a minute.

The second thing that I need to make clear is that annual goals don't have to start on January 1st. Yes, once you get into a groove and start feeling comfortable about goal setting, it makes sense to plan your goals out from year to year, beginning with January 1st. That's what I do. Every December 31st, I reflect on my previous year, review my progress, and chart the new year ahead, all while aiming at my five-year goal.

But for now, I want you to imagine that tomorrow is January 1st. If you're not quite ready to start setting annual goals, that's okay, too. If you plan on starting your annual goal-setting next week, pretend that day is January 1st. The point is, don't get hung up on thinking that annual goals need to start on January 1st, because they don't.

You don't have to start setting your annual goals today if

Four Universal Goals to Start Setting Today

you're not ready, but whatever you do, don't read this book, return it to your shelf, and tell yourself that you'll begin setting goals on January 1st. Trust me; if you're excited about what goal setting can do for your life, you don't want to waste time in waiting for New Years Day.

If today is April 15th, August 12th, October 23rd, or any other day of the year, think about what you can do by April 15th, August 12th, or October 23rd of next year to get closer to your long-term goals. What can you do to move the needle on your long-term goals in the next 365 days?

You don't have to think in terms of vast, year-long tasks, either. Annual goals can come in one of two forms: 1) goals that may take an entire year to see realized, or 2) a handful of smaller goals that you're going to tackle quarter by quarter. I want to talk about both because they often go hand-in-hand.

What You Can Accomplish in One Year Might Surprise You

When I started thinking about my five-year vision, I started making a list of everything I would need to do to make it a reality.

If I wanted to start speaking to audiences about goal-setting, what could I do to establish myself as an expert? Start a blog. Write a book. Start talking to small groups.

If I wanted to make enough money for Callie to quit her job, what could I do in the coming year? Open an IRA. Start a blog. Write a book. Pay off some debt. Start a 9-month emergency fund.

If I wanted to improve my health and wellness, what could I do in the coming year? Improve my cardiovascular health. Run a half-marathon. Start eating more vegetables and heart-healthy grains.

The list could go on and on, but don't let that overwhelm you. Working towards a five-year plan is going to take approximately five years. (Duh, right?)

You don't have to do everything on your five-year list in the first 365 days. The aim is to identify everything you need to do so that you can choose what to do in the next year. You can't do everything all at once. And don't worry, the worksheets that accompany this chapter will guide you through this process.

As you already know, I started working towards my five-year dream by starting my blog, Daily New Year's. I began building the website in October of 2017 and launched in June of 2018. After my launch I focused on writing new blog posts for a full year. In the first year, I wrote fifty unique blog posts, roughly one per week, and I started the podcast some time in the middle of the year.

Then on December 31, 2018, I looked back at my five-year vision and evaluated what I should do next. The idea for my book was calling me. I had a year and a half of writing experience under my belt and felt like 2019 was as good a time as any, so I made this book one of my 2019 annual goals.

Writing a book may seem like one big, year-long goal that would leave time for nothing else, but several other goals were competing for my time in 2019 as well. In fact, it's not uncommon for me to have ten to twenty annual goals per year.

For example, I set goals to run a half-marathon, write this book, remodel the den in my house, build a deck, develop a new website for Element 74, just to name a few. I have career goals, personal goals, relationship goals, household goals—it's a lot to juggle. We'll get more into avoiding goal competition and how to prioritize in later chapters.

For now, it's important to note that not all annual goals need to take a full year to complete. I didn't plan on spending 365 days working on any one of these goals. Some of these goals were going to take all year, but others might take six months or two weeks. The durations vary, but the trick is to plan your year and avoid working towards all of your goals simultaneously.

It's difficult to write a book, train for a half marathon, hold down a forty-hour-a-week career, remodel a room in your house, and write a new blog post every week. You can't do everything at once. That's why I stagger my larger goals across quarters.

Queue Up the Quarterly Goals

Often, annual goals are not one big thing that you work towards all year long. I believe that is why New Year's resolutions fail; they're one big, ambiguous goal. Instead, annual goals are often comprised of dozens of smaller goals that you can stack strategically throughout the year.

Take writing this book. I didn't start by saying, "I'm going to write a book this year." That's far too big and vague. We have to break our annual goals down. So instead, in one quarter, I decided to write the rough draft of my book, start training for a half-marathon, and put my blog and podcast on ice.

The next quarter, I continued my half-marathon training while I worked to edit, revise, and polish the book. In the next ninety days, I might publish, promote, and begin selling my book. With the half-marathon behind me, I can start remodeling my house and building my deck.

Now I know, you're probably not writing a book or building a deck. My examples are pretty specific, but the point is, the key to annual and quarterly goals is to break things down and strategically decide on what to work on now and what to put on hold for later.

Putting my blog on hold for well over three months was extremely difficult for me to do. I had spent eighteen months working on it week after week. But for the book to be a success, I couldn't fragment my time; I had to put the blog on hold.

As you look to your five-year dream, what goals are most important for you to complete this year? From there, break it down. What do you need to do first? Second? Third?

Start charting it out on paper. Use the notes pages and worksheets that accompany this chapter to help you along. If you're starting this process right in the middle of the third quarter, identify your Q3 goals based on the time you have left. Then move on to Q4.

When December 31st rolls around, you can reassess and start with Q1 of next year, but whatever you do, DO NOT wait for that day to start planning out your quarterly goals.

Regardless of when you're starting this planning process, remember that quarterly goals are specifically designed to move you closer to your annual goals, so don't lose focus. Aim at your annual goals.

Now you may be wondering, "How many quarterly goals should I have?" Great question! It varies, depending on what you're trying to accomplish, but it's best not to pursue more than three to five goals per quarter. Personally, I like to have a few personal goals and a couple of professional goals each quarter.

Once your annual and quarterly goals begin to take shape, we can move on to the other three types of goals. These goals break things down even further, giving us daily and weekly action goals, habit goals, and achievement goals.

3. Action Goals

You've got your five-year, annual, and quarterly goals all charted out and written down, right? Are you starting to get excited or overwhelmed?

Don't worry; we're going to continue to refine and simplify this process by breaking it down further. We're talking about several different types of goals in this chapter, but it helps to remember that all of these goals work to support each other.

We're not learning four different types of goals to keep track of or to choose from; we're essentially learning four ways to crush our life's biggest goals. Everything we're learning is helping to move us towards those long-term goals by breaking those larger goals down into the smallest, actionable pieces.

If you're anything like me, you've probably packed each quarter with a healthy, but challenging, set of goals. But to achieve success, we have to distill each quarterly goal into a list of action goals. Think of this as your ninety-day to-do list.

Once you have your quarterly goals in place, make a chronological list of every action you need to take to complete your goal. Your list could be five steps, or a hundred, depending on your goal. It may take a while, but try to write down every single thing you need to do. If any step seems too big, try to break it down further.

When you do this for each of your quarterly goals, these lists become your action goals, and they are the roadmap for crushing your quarterly goals.

Once you have these lists, store them in a place that you can refer to often. We'll get to how to track your goals in a later chapter, but when you keep these lists of action goals, you give yourself a road map to refer back to daily, if needed.

Day after day and week after week, you can work towards these action goals knowing that, once everything is complete, you will have achieved your quarterly goal.

4. Habit Goals

The last of the four types of goals I want to share with you is the habit goal. This one is probably my favorite because habits are at the core of any good routine, and I love a good routine!

Habit goals allow us to break our larger goals down into daily or weekly habits. For example, on my blog, I wanted to release one new post per week, so I formed a habit of writing every Monday night after work. That's a weekly habit.

I also wanted to make sure I made room for exercise in my schedule for my fitness goals, so I developed a habit of waking up at 4:45 a.m. every weekday to make room for exercise. Boom! Daily habit.

In 2016 I wanted to get into my local gym's 1,250-pound club, so I had to lift 5 days a week without fail and monitor my progress and diet closely. Before that, I once wanted to cycle a century [4], so I had to train for that 5 to 6 times per week. Currently, I'm signed up for a half-marathon, and you guessed it, I have to prepare for that, too. All of these goals are easier to achieve by building habits around the result.

Habit Goals are a way of taking larger goals and breaking them into more manageable, sustainable pieces. If you want to run a marathon, you wouldn't sign up and run it the next day; you would begin running several times per week and build towards your success.

---

    4 A century is a one hundred-mile bike ride. I did one called the Tour de Corn, though I don't remember seeing many corn fields.

Four Universal Goals to Start Setting Today

Unlike most goals, habit goals don't have to be measurable or specific. I picked up the concept of habit goals from Michael Hyatt. He uses the example of "Growing closer to God," [13] which is vague, yet aspirational.

"Growing closer to God" or deepening your spiritual connections are not measurable goals, but you could set a habit of reading your Bible, meditating, praying, or however else you worship within your own faith and work towards that goal daily.

While habit goals don't have to be measurable or specific, they can be. If you want to write a book, you could set a habit goal to write five hundred words per day. If you're going to read twelve books per year, you could set a habit goal to read a set number of pages per day.

We can use habit goals to establish routines that we design with our larger goals in mind. Essentially, habit goals allow us to automate our success by tracking daily habits.

Most people know of Jerry Seinfeld. He's the comedian behind the most successful sitcom in history, *Seinfeld*, and he's a hugely successful comedian. It's easy to believe that he was born with a gift, perhaps even an oversized funny bone. But he started the same way we all do: at the bottom.

As an up and coming comedian, he wanted to write better, funnier jokes. Like many before him, Seinfeld concluded that the secret to quality was quantity. Writing more jokes would eventually lead to funnier jokes, so he needed to write every day.

To keep himself accountable, Seinfeld would start each year with a blank, year-at-a-glance calendar hanging on his wall. For every day that he wrote new material, he would place a large, red X through that day.

Seinfeld shared his advice with software developer Brad Isaac. He told Brad:

> "After a few days you'll have a chain. Just keep at it, and the chain will grow longer every day. You'll like seeing that chain, especially when you get a few weeks under your belt. Your only job next is to not break the chain. Don't break the chain."

Seinfeld attributes his success to this "Don't break the chain" technique, which if you look closely, is nothing more than a well-established habit goal. If Seinfeld can use habit goals to become one of the most successful comedians in the world, what could you achieve by using habit goals?

The possibilities are endless and may even surprise you.

Start at the Top

Like I said at the beginning of this chapter, there are countless types of goals out there, from SMART goals, Big Hairy Audacious Goals, Twenty-Five-Year Visions, and everything in between. But there's no need to get bogged down with too many complex concepts.

As you begin to set goals for yourself, think about what you want your life to be like in five years. Practice some Blue-Sky Thinking and then start writing down some goals that will help get you closer to that dream.

If it helps, run your goals through **The FOCUSED Framework** to ensure your goals are ones that you're genuinely excited to pursue over the long haul.

After that, start breaking your long-term goals down into annual and quarterly goals and build in action and habit goals to help you succeed day after day.

Four Universal Goals to Start Setting Today

Remember, the tiniest action goal or daily habit should build towards your quarterly and annual goals, which should in turn build towards your long-term goals. We're not trying to set hundreds of goals to keep track of; we're trying to take a handful of long-term goals and break them down into manageable pieces.

In other words, start at the top and work your way down towards the daily and weekly actions you need to take to see your goals realized. Makes sense, right?

As simple as that sounds, it can still be easy to get overwhelmed with the day-to-day list of things you need to do. Wake up early, go to the gym, read for thirty minutes, write five hundred words, go to work, check in on your career goals, make time for family—it can be daunting! Who has the time?

Look, I hear you. It does seem like a lot to manage, but don't worry, in the next chapter I'm going to give you a handful of strategies that I use to keep my time prioritized so that I can make meaningful progress on my goals.

Using a couple of simple prioritization techniques, I'll show you how you can get far more done in significantly less time than you ever thought possible.

CHAPTER RECAP

Key Takeaways

- **Long-Term Goals** are any goals you want to achieve over the course of your life and **Annual Goals** are the larger goals that will help you achieve your long-term life goals.

- **Annual goals are not resolutions.** Resolutions are born of good intentions, but seldom pan out in the end due to the synthetic motivation that burns out quickly.

- **Blue-Sky Thinking** is the practice of looking forward into your future and imagining that all things are possible for you, that you have no limits to speak of, and that your life is perfect in every way.

- The concept behind Blue-Sky Thinking is not to trick your mind into jumping from A to Z overnight; the idea is to remove all of the limits in your mind so that you can truly see what's possible in life.

- **Quarterly Goals** are the goals that help keep you on track for your annual goals. You can have several quarterly goals across all areas of your life, from professional to personal and from family to fitness.

- **Action Goals** are all of the tasks and actions you must take to achieve your quarterly goals. Think of this as your goal-driven to-do list.

- **Habit Goals** allow us to break larger goals down into daily or weekly actions that help us to form habits and routines around our goals. You can use habit goals to help automate your success.

- Remember, the tiniest action goal or daily habit should build towards your quarterly and annual goals which should, in turn, build towards your long-term goals.

Four Universal Goals to Start Setting Today

Memorable Quotes

☆ *"Only you can determine what's possible for you."*

☆ *"Don't break the chain."* —Jerry Seinfeld

Put it into Practice

- Using the accompanying worksheets, plan your 3- to 5-year vision. This will be your launch pad for setting your annual goals.
- ☐ Using your 3- to 5-year vision, plan out your annual and quarterly achievement goals. What do you need to achieve this year to get closer to your vision?
- ☐ If any of your quarterly goals could benefit from building a habit, use the 66-day habit goals worksheets to track your progress.
- ☐ Track and journal your progress every day!

Prioritize Like a Pro & Crush Your Goals in Record Time

"Most of us spend too much time on what is urgent and not enough time on what is important."

– Stephen R. Covey

If there's only one thing every goal-driven person should know for sure, it's how to prioritize. If you can't effectively prioritize your time or your tasks, your goals will take a back seat to less important things.

We've all been there: you wake up in the morning, grab a cup of coffee, and head into the office with the tenacity to get some significant work done only to come home later that day feeling like you accomplished absolutely NOTHING.

I've been there, and I know you have, too—everyone has! It sucks!

Occasionally, I go through spells where I find myself having more of these unpredictable days, and honestly, it bums me out. I don't enjoy feeling unproductive, especially when I recall times when I was cranking away and getting meaningful, deep work done.

In most cases, we allow ourselves to become distracted with shallow work, empty conversations, and fruitless endeavors. When I fall into this trap, I dig deep and remind myself of several principles and practices that help me prioritize. In this chapter, we're going to talk about:

- Time Blocking
- The Four Ds of Task Management
- Pareto's Principle, aka the 80/20 Rule
- The Eisenhower Matrix
- The ABCDE Method

Each technique serves me in different ways, so when I get overwhelmed or feel unproductive, I lean on the one that I find most useful for the situation. In this chapter, I'm going to explain how each one of these methods works and how it can serve you in your goal setting.

Time Blocking

Do you ever feel like your days get away from you in a flash?

You go to work with a plan, but then everyone else's emergencies become your top priorities? I struggle with this from time to time because it's a tricky trap to avoid, but for the most part, I use time blocking to combat the busyness.

Not so long ago, I was a Project Manager at the website development company that I still work at today. Back in the project management days, I was in charge of me, myself, and I. I worked with a team of freelance designers and internal developers who worked to meet deadlines that we set for our collective clients. For the most part, I was in control of my schedule and my productive output. I could come in, put my head down, and focus on laying out pages for days. Sure, I would have the occasional last-minute meeting or I would need to help someone with a quick problem, but for the most part, I was left to do my work.

Flash forward several years later, and I would find myself serving the company in more ways that one: I was leading an agile website development team, I was a member of the company's leadership team, I ran our marketing and business development initiatives, and I oversaw the production of a YouTube channel for a client that released three to four episodes per week.

I don't tell you all of this to brag—I'm the first to admit that I didn't want to wear four or five different hats. But I work for a relatively small company, and many of us wear a variety of hats. I tell you all of this for one reason: I would not have survived my many roles if it were not for time blocking!

What is Time Blocking?

Time blocks, simply put, are blocks of time that you plan out in advance to get your top priority tasks done without interruption.

Let's say you have a presentation due this Friday and it's going to take a considerable amount of time. You could approach it a couple of different ways.

You could field every question, every task, and every emergency that comes your way, putting your presentation off until the end of the day. Then you stay late every night and do a less-than-amazing job because you're tired, burnt out, and behind schedule.

OR

Crush Your Goals!

You could sit down on Monday morning and schedule several blocks of time on your calendar reserved explicitly for your presentation, making it your top priority. You could shut your door, work remotely, turn off your email, shut down Slack, and silence your phone—whatever it takes to avoid distraction or interruption, and get your presentation completed and polished.

Which option sounds better to you? The second one, right?

Intentionally reserving time for priority tasks and projects is the essence of time blocking, and it's powerful. I use time blocking for my morning gym routine, my content creation sessions for my blog and podcast, my lunch breaks, and so much more.

Brendon Burchard says that he can tell what's important to a person just by looking at their calendar and he's right.

If you were to see my schedule, you would see that I'm devoted to my blog, this book, and my health because I reserve time for all of those things. It's all there in beautiful little blocks of intentional time.

But you're probably thinking, "Easier said than done. There's no way I can just shut everything out." I thought the same thing at first, but over time, you can change both your habits and the habits of the people around you.

Today, it's common for me to disappear to a coffee shop for hours on end. I'll use a focus app to block distracting apps and websites for an hour at a time, but I always check in with the people who need me before and after each block. But that's during the workday.

For my personal goals, I wake up as early as I can, often before five a.m. so that I can focus on my blog, book, fitness, or anything else that I find essential.

Time blocking is possible; it just requires a change in your daily habits and routines. Yes, waking up early is hard, especially at first, and it's hard to block out coworkers and other distractions, but it's worth it when you can use this technique to get your most meaningful work done.

If you're willing to give it a try, let's take a look at some of the specifics, such as time block duration and how you can use them to tackle your goals.

How Long Should Time Blocks Be?

I've personally read several different articles on the correct length of time blocks. According to the Technique [1], it's twenty-five minute blocks separated by short breaks. According to this technique, twenty-five minutes is long enough to be productive but short enough to avoid becoming exhausted.

I've been writing this chapter for well over twenty-five minutes and don't feel like twenty-five minutes is long enough for me to be productive.

I've also read that ninety-minute blocks are appropriate, but I would argue that it is a tad too long. I need a coffee break more often than that.

The third model I've read about is one you may be familiar with: fifty minutes of focused work and then a ten-minute break. If this seems familiar, you may recall that high school and college courses are often set up this way, and I find that fifty minutes is the perfect amount of time to get some

---

1 The Pomodoro Technique is a time management method developed by Francesco Cirillo in the late 1980s. The technique uses a timer to break down work into intervals, traditionally twenty-five minutes in length, separated by short breaks. Each interval is known as a pomodoro, from the Italian word for tomato, after the tomato-shaped kitchen timer that Cirillo used as a university student.

significant work done.

The time may vary for you, so I recommend experimenting with it. If you start getting fidgety twenty-five minutes into a block, don't try to push through. Your focus will begin to diminish anyway, so jump up and take a five-minute break.

If you're at fifty minutes and you're still in the zone, maybe you're a ninety-minute kind of person. Be careful, though. You might feel like a ninety-minute kind of person in the morning, but find yourself utterly fatigued in the afternoon, leaving your productivity on empty.

Time-blocking is about sustaining productivity and energy so that you can get more significant work done and so that you can make time for your goals. The last thing you want to do is have a highly productive morning and a zombie-like afternoon. That's not going to help you crush your goals; trust me.

Now that I've thoroughly explained time blocking, I want to share some examples of how you can use it. This technique is not just for large tasks that fit perfectly into fifty-minute blocks. You can use time blocking to group several small tasks together in a batch, to tackle large tasks, or to chip away at a massive project with multiple milestones.

Small, Batched Tasks

Some of the biggest time wasters we all encounter every day are actually pretty tiny by nature. Most emails only take seconds to read. Responding is pretty quick, too. Checking a notification here and there only takes a minute or two, right? Wrong!

As harmless as they may seem, these tiny tasks have more potential to waste our days than anything else because these interruptions can add up.

According to estimates based on a recent UC Irvine study, it can take up to twenty-three minutes to refocus your attention to an original task after a single interruption. That same study found that the average worker switched tasks on average every three minutes. Task switching saps enormous amounts of time and energy and is the complete opposite of time blocking.

If allowed, these not-so-tiny tasks can rob us of our days, leaving no time to pursue our more meaningful goals. That's why I like to group smaller things into a single time block. Here's an example of one of my fifty-minute blocks:

- Catch up on my inbox using the Four Ds: Do it, Defer it, Delete it, or Delegate it.
- Check and respond to Slack messages.
- Respond to any calls or voicemails that I may have.

These are all related to communication in one way or another, so it makes sense to batch them. Separately and scattered throughout the day, these messages can steal large amounts of time, but batched, I can move through them in an easy fifty minutes or less.

Once complete, I shut these channels down until my next communication block. It takes practice, but you can do it, too. Once you've managed to rescue vast portions of your day from distracting communication, you can begin to use your time blocks for larger tasks.

Large, Single-Block Tasks

What constitutes a large task? For me, it can mean a lot of things. At work, more often than not, large tasks usually take the form of meetings, drafting proposals, writing and reviewing contracts, calculating sales figures, and so on. But for you, your large tasks could be any number of things. The key is that they should typically fit into one of your time blocks. For me, that's fifty minutes.

Take meetings, for example. It's best to limit most meetings to fifty to sixty minutes because conversations will expand to fill excess time anyway. Trust me; if you know you have two hours to fill, you'll fill the time with unimportant conversations. When you limit your time, you use the time more efficiently. That being the case, why not limit meetings to fifty minutes?

Meetings are just one example. The main thing is to keep the time block intact. If you often find yourself expanding your time blocks to fit the work, you might be trying to cram massive projects into chunks of time that were designed for tasks and smaller milestones.

Huge, Milestone-Driven Projects

If you have a project or task that is too big for one fifty-minute block, don't try to force your way through it in one sitting. For me, these types of projects could be writing a blog, publishing a podcast, building a website, or even something as massive as writing this book.

Instead of pushing through, break your project into chunks. Here's how I tackle my weekly blog, podcast, and social media schedule using fifty-minute blocks of time:

- ⊘ Monday morning, I post an inspirational quote and create three more quotes to use throughout the week.
- ⊘ Monday evening, I outline and draft a new blog post, breaking the session into three 50-minute blocks with short breaks in between, one for dinner.
- ⊘ Tuesday morning, I review my draft with fresh

eyes and make revisions, adding images and graphics as I go.
- ⊘ Tuesday at lunch, I record a new episode of the podcast.
- ⊘ Tuesday evening, I edit the podcast, draft the show notes, and create the social media graphics, using several blocks to do so.
- ⊘ Wednesday morning, I post the podcast to my social channels and engage with the community.
- ⊘ Thursday I prep my blog post for the Friday launch by creating the email and the social post graphics and captions.
- ⊘ Friday I send the email and upload the posts to my social channels.

Sounds like a pretty scattered week, wouldn't you say? I'm sure many of you would be tempted to cram most of this into one or two different days, perhaps using the weekends. It might seem more effective to push through and do as much in one sitting as possible. I used to do it this way, and I wasn't fond of the outcome.

I found that when I would sit down and do all of this at once on a Saturday, I would become exhausted, overwhelmed, and my quality would suffer. Not to mention, I wouldn't get to use my Saturdays for other things such as home projects or family time.

Time blocking allows me to stay consistent and fresh with my content week after week, day after day. It may be a slower pace overall, but spreading the work out and resting in between keeps me going longer with more considerable energy.

Sure, I could cram my entire production schedule into a single day, but while I'm still working a full-time job, time blocking allows me to maintain high performance while also sustaining my energy for the long haul.

When it comes to your big goals, maintaining your energy and enthusiasm are vital to your long-term success. Time blocking is a great way to do that, but remember, your blocks don't have to be fifty minutes. Your blocks could follow the twenty-five-minute Pomodoro technique, or they could be ninety minutes long. The only way to find out what's best for you is to get started.

Getting Started with Time Blocking

Now that you know what time blocking is, and assuming I've sold you on the strategy, it's time to implement it into your life. Here's how: assuming you've already taken your long-term goals and broken them down into annual and quarterly goals, start with your goals for the week ahead.

Sit down on Monday morning and review your major projects, pre-committed appointments, and goals and ask yourself: "If I could get three significant things done this week, what would they be?" The answer to this question will become your weekly Big Three.

Then map out three blocks of time each day that move the needle on those big three goals. These will become your daily Big Three. Other than meetings you may already have scheduled, these blocks are not intended for spontaneous meetings, email, communication, etc.—they're strictly meant for your weekly Big Three.

Now, make sure to leave one or two blocks for email and communication and find the optimal time for batching those tasks. For me, contrary to many studies, I find that first thing in the morning works best. I also check in again in the early afternoon.

Finally, commit these to your calendar and guard this time. People will ask you to compromise, to cancel or reschedule your priority tasks for their tasks, and they'll try to convince you that their tasks are urgent or more important than your own. It can be difficult to know when to defend your time versus when to make the compromise, and there are times when you need to do both, but it's okay to give yourself permission to defend both your time and your priorities.

Saying no, deferring a request until later, and protecting your priorities can be challenging at first, but you can't always allow someone else's emergencies to become your top priorities. (Now, I'm coming at this from a professional, job-based perspective. If someone around you is experiencing a true emergency, or if a loved one needs your help with something important, it's okay to drop what you're doing and lend a hand. Let's all be good humans.)

There will always be countless things capable of consuming your time, and if allowed, these things will multiply. If you say yes to every request that comes your way, you will become the person that everyone begins to dump tasks on, leaving your priorities left undone and your goals unaccomplished.

Lastly, don't leave your daily Big Three goals unchecked; review them at the beginning and end of each day. Did you get everything done? If not, do you need to juggle some things around for tomorrow? What caused you to miss completing your Big Three today?

These are things to consider as you move forward because not every day will be perfect. You won't always crush your Big Three. If you didn't achieve one of your Big Three today, should it be your top priority tomorrow? Can you juggle your time blocks around to accommodate the missed deadline, or will you have to push something else off until next week?

Time Blocking is a powerful tool for crushing our goals, but it's not a magic bullet that will solve all of our problems. Even after we've scheduled our priorities, we'll eventually have to reprioritize. As new tasks, variables, deadlines, and other things enter the mix, we'll have to reevaluate our goals continuously.

For this constant reevaluation and reprioritization, we'll need to learn several other strategies starting with the Four Ds.

The Four Ds

In today's fast-paced, communication-driven world, our inboxes and to-do lists tend to fill up quickly, and it can be tough to know what to work on first.

I've seen people start each day at the top of their inboxes, working on whatever is newest first. As soon as a new email comes in, they abandon whatever it was that they were working on for the new thing that just arrived.

This behavior can leave important tasks buried far below their ever-growing pile of emails. I've seen other people do the exact opposite, leaving important messages unanswered for days.

The same situation applies to our to-do lists. Many of us keep a running list of all the things we've been asked to do, and we do our best to stay on top of it. Often times, though, it's tempting to start working on the newest thing that just jumped on the list via the coffee pot run-in we just had with our boss.

Again, it can be challenging to know what to work on first, especially when things are coming at us from a hundred different directions.

The fact is (and get ready for this one), not everything is worth doing. Some things need to be deleted, and some need to be done by someone else entirely. Some are so quick and easy that it's tempting to jump on them right away. Should we give in and just knock these things out? Maybe, but not always.

The Four Ds are a straightforward framework for dealing with these types of situations. Essentially, they are four phrases that can help us determine what to do with a task or an email: Delete It, Do It, Defer It, or Delegate It.

Sounds easy, right? In theory, the Four Ds are easy to learn; the challenge can be in combining them with time blocking, putting them into practice, and sticking to them. While the Four Ds can be used independently from time blocking and can be helpful in everyday decision making, I often find myself using them together. To help illustrate the power of the Four Ds, I'm going to run through an example time-block designed for email or task management. With this process we can quickly and effectively move through our inboxes and to-do lists, clearing our path for our more important work.

To get started, designate a single, uninterrupted block of time for clearing email or sprinting through your to-do list. The goal here is not to get hung up on any one item or to work on things in sequential order. The goal is email and to-do list reduction. Are you ready? Let's go!

Delete It

Deleting tasks from your inbox or to-do list is by far the quickest and easiest, and that's why I've placed it first.

When you dive into your first time block, go through your to-do list or your inbox and delete everything that is unimportant.

For email, don't get distracted by email offers, sales, or coupons—delete everything that is going to waste your time.

If you want to shorten this step for future weeks, start

unsubscribing or blocking as many junk emails as you can so you don't have to keep dealing with them week after week. It takes a little extra time on the front end, but it's going to reduce your junk email over the long term.

For your to-do list, delete anything that is no longer important. Perhaps something landed on your to-do list several weeks ago, and it no longer needs to be done. If so, just erase it or mark it out.

If you're unsure of a task or email's importance, or if everything seems important, don't worry! We're going to learn how to determine importance using a few different techniques later in this chapter.

For now, know that deleting all of the unimportant items first will clear your path for the more important things on your list.

Do It

Once you've eliminated all of the unnecessary tasks or emails, use the remainder of your time block to start working on all of the tasks that take five minutes or less.

Five minutes is the key here. Because you're in a time block meant for task or email reduction, the goal is not to complete large projects.

For every five-minute task you eliminate, you have one less thing weighing on your mind or preventing you from working towards your weekly goals.

Defer It

As you work through your to-do list or inbox, you're going to come across tasks and emails that are too big to tackle at that moment because they're longer than five minutes.

When this happens, you need to defer those tasks. Take a second to create a time block on your calendar to specifically deal with that task or project at a later date.

Maybe an email comes in asking you to put together a report for an upcoming meeting. Don't abandon your current time block to pursue that task. Instead, figure out how many time blocks that job is going to take and put them on your calendar. Once you've deferred the task, continue through your list.

Delegate It

As you sort through your to-do list or inbox, keep in mind that not all tasks need to be done by you specifically. If you're in management, ask yourself, "Could one of my direct reports do this at a lower cost for the company?" for each of the tasks that you come across. The rate of pay and hierarchy are important here. Depending on where you fall in your organization or company, there could be highly capable people under you that should be doing some of these tasks on your to-do list, but at a lower rate for the company. Asking your reports to take on some of your smaller tasks will allow you to focus on the larger duties that you've most likely been assigned.

If you're just starting out in your career, or if you don't have any direct reports, try asking yourself, "Does someone else have the bandwidth or availability to take this off of my plate?" Just because you're starting out or are new to the organization doesn't mean you have to do everything on your own to the point of burnout or exhaustion. In this case, delegation is more like asking for help.

Delegation isn't about ditching your duties or getting someone else to do your work, but if your job is to move the organization forward by completing high-level activities, such as acquiring new customers, you probably shouldn't be ordering new pens or putting new toner in the printer. Not that those tasks aren't necessary or important, but they might be more in line with someone else's job description or bandwidth.

So if you find these types of tasks in your inbox or on your to-do list, assign them to someone else or ask for help. Politely ask the person capable of the job to take care of it for you. Once you've delegated the task, move on to your more essential projects and time blocks.

Wrapping Up

At the end of this email or to-do list reduction time block, you should have completed several small tasks, scheduled other large tasks for a later date, delegated some of your work to your reports or colleagues, and deleted work that is no longer important to you or your overall mission.

In a very short amount of time, your list should have shrunk significantly, but this was just one time block and one example of how you might use the Four Ds to maximize your productivity.

Now, let's look at the Four Ds over time.

Are the Four Ds Effective Long Term?

Now that you've learned the Four Ds you might be wondering if they work long term.

The Four Ds are a tried and true method for streamlining and optimizing the process of task and email management, but they work best when you practice discipline and time blocking. Without those two things, it's far too easy to fall back into the frantic game of whack-a-mole that keeps derailing your productivity.

Depending on how many requests you have coming at you, it may take more than one time block per day to apply the Four Ds to your inbox or to-do list. For email, I do this once in the morning and then again in the early afternoon. For my to-do list, I apply the Four Ds once a week or every other week. The process keeps my lists and inboxes clean and my priorities straight.

Once I know I've dealt with all of the quick tasks and scheduled or deferred everything else, I can focus my efforts on my most important goals and my weekly and daily Big Three.

As I mentioned earlier, it's not always easy to determine what is most important, especially at a glance. Which tasks should we delete? Which tasks should we do first? When there are not enough hours in the week, which things should win in the competition for our time?

To answer that, we need to look at Pareto's Principle.

Pareto's Principle, aka the 80/20 Rule

Often referred to as the 80/20 Rule, Pareto's Principle states that, for many events, roughly 80 percent of the effects come from 20 percent of the causes. [14] In other words, for most things, 80 percent of your rewards are going to come from 20 percent of your efforts. Here are some examples:

- ✓ In business, it is common for 80 percent of a company's sales or revenue will come from 20 percent of its clients.
- ✓ It is estimated that approximately 20 percent of the world's population controls a little over 80 percent of the world's income. [15]
- ✓ To use a more specific example, Microsoft found that they could eliminate 80 percent of their crashes by fixing the top 20 percent of reported

bugs.[16]

If you do some research, you'll find countless examples of the 80/20 rule in action, but what's important to understand is that this rule also applies to your daily efforts.

When you're examining the list of all the things that you could do, it helps to identify which 20 percent of those things will have the most significant, overall impact.

If I'm in sales and my goal is to close a certain amount of new business, which of these is going to have a more substantial impact on that goal:

1. Completing a proposal on time, presenting that proposal to a new client, and closing a deal, or
2. Responding to sixty-seven insignificant emails, answering the phone every time it rings, and having spontaneous "meetings" with my colleagues in the hallway?

When you look at it that way, the answer seems pretty clear and easy to prioritize. However, as we move throughout our days and attempt to keep our to-do lists as short as possible, we often fail to prioritize correctly.

Most of us want to close out our to-do lists, so we strive to get everything done. We hope to clear our plates today so that we might focus on our goals tomorrow. But getting everything done is impossible!

Starting tomorrow with a clean slate is a beautiful dream, but it's not one that you're likely to see come true. You see, for every task we complete, two more pop up to take its place. This cycle is a game we cannot win unless we change the rules.

Using Pareto's Principle and the concept the 80/20 rule, we

can shift our focus from trying to do everything on our list to only focusing on the precious 20 percent of tasks that will move the needle the most. However, for this strategy to work successfully, we have to learn how to identify which things are important and which ones only seem to be important.

The challenge is differentiating between urgent and important, and that's where the Eisenhower Matrix comes into play.

The Eisenhower Matrix

One of my favorite ways to prioritize my tasks is by using the Eisenhower Matrix, but before we learn how to use the matrix, let's look at the difference between urgent tasks and important tasks.

Urgent tasks are those that seem to scream "NOW!" and they put us in a state of reaction. If you ever feel like you run from one fire to another all day long, you know what I mean.

Important tasks are the ones that contribute to your long-term goals. These can be urgent, but they seldom are. President Dwight D. Eisenhower had a successful career and was known to use this method, hence the name. Here's what he said: "What is important is seldom urgent, and what is urgent is seldom important."

What Eisenhower said is true. When something is important, we often know about it well in advance, so we've planned for it ahead of time. If you sign up for a marathon, you understand that training is essential. Therefore, you would schedule your training around that goal beginning several months before race day. You wouldn't feel a sense of urgency around training unless you put it off until the last minute. (Been there, done that!)

In that example, training for the marathon is important in

either case; it only becomes urgent if you ignore your plan or fail to plan altogether. What is important is seldom urgent, and what is urgent is rarely important.

Okay, now that we know the difference between urgent and important, let's take a look at a simple but effective framework for determining a task's importance. I hope you got an A in art class because this framework is going to take some serious skill.

I'm kidding! All we have to do is draw a two-by-two square grid. You can do this in your daily planner or on a scrap piece of paper; it's totally up to you.

First, draw a large square about four or five inches in both directions, then divide it into equal quadrants. Across the top two squares write "urgent" and "not urgent." Next, write "important" and "not important" down the left side boxes, like so:

	Urgent	**Not Urgent**
Important	Do It	Defer It
Not Important	Delegate It	Delete It

Finally, take your entire to-do list and dump it into these four squares. But before you do, remember that not everything is equal. Some things are much more important than the others, so keep the 80/20 rule in mind. As you evaluate each task, ask things like:

- Does this task move the needle on my larger goals?
- Could someone else do this?
- Does this have to be done right now, or could I do it later?
- What would happen if I were to never complete this task?

These types of questions can help you determine which quadrant to dump a task into. For example, answering "yes" to the first question means the task is important. Answering "yes" to the second question means you should delegate the task.

Answering "I can do this later" to the third question implies that the task is not urgent. And, if you said "nothing" to the last question, the task is probably not important or urgent.

These aren't the only questions you could use to evaluate which quadrant a task should go into, but they're great questions for getting started. If you'd like, be sure to add your own evaluative questions as needed.

Once you're done placing your to-do list into the squares, you can apply the Four Ds to the squares. Here's what you do:

- If your tasks are urgent and important, do them first.
- If your tasks are not urgent but they are important, defer them for later. Go ahead and schedule them if you need to.

- If they're urgent but they're not important, delegate them to someone else.
- If they're not urgent and not important, delete them from your list—trust me; they aren't worth doing at all.

As you can see, not everything on your list is something you have to do, and you most certainly don't have to do everything right this instant. Once you've delegated a portion of your list and deleted another portion, you can get back to working on what's truly important to your goals.

Not a fan of sketching squares? That's okay. I want to close out the chapter with one last strategy for prioritizing your to-do list that doesn't require any art skills—you just need to know your ABCs.

The ABCDE Method of Prioritization

If the Eisenhower Matrix seems like a bit too much work with all the doodling, you could use the ABCDE Method instead. I picked this method up from Brian Tracy's book Goals!

To use this method, you assign a letter to each of your tasks. According to Tracy's book, the framework looks like this:

A—These tasks are critical and have high consequences. Getting them done should be your top priority because these tasks contribute the most to your long-term success.

B—These tasks have smaller consequences, though they are still important, such as answering email.

C—These tasks would be good to do, but they have no consequence on your life at all. Nothing terrible will happen if these items are never completed.

D—"D" is for Delegate. These are the tasks that should be done by someone else so that you can focus on the big picture.

E—"E" is for Eliminate. These tasks are not worth doing at all by anyone. As your goals progress, evolve, or change completely, many old tasks become unimportant. Just because they were on your list at one point does not mean you still have to do them today.

There you have it! Learning how to prioritize is as simple as knowing your ABCs. Anything beyond a C isn't something you should be doing.

Personally, I prefer using the Eisenhower Matrix in combination with the Four Ds because I'm a visual learner. But perhaps you prefer the simplicity of the ABCDE Method. There's no right or wrong way to prioritize your tasks or your goals. The important thing is to try each of them and then use what works for you.

Now that I've armed you with time blocking, the Four Ds, Pareto's Principle, the Eisenhower Matrix, and the ABCDE Method, you have everything you need to prioritize like a pro!

Like anything, using these methods will take practice. The more you use them, the faster and better you'll get at weeding through your daily tasks. After a while, you'll have built a powerful new habit that will serve you and your goals for years to come.

The Eternal To-Do List

Before we move on, I want to repeat a thought from earlier in the chapter: your to-do list will never be empty. Even with the powerful tools found in this chapter, you will still have a finite amount of time each day. You'll have to decide which things to do today and which things to leave for later.

The point of the strategies found in this chapter is not to help you clear your to-do list; they're designed to help you balance your day so that you have time for focusing on your most important goals. Creating six, 50-minute time blocks per day won't help you crush your goals if you use all six blocks to get ahead of your inbox.

On the other hand, working on your big goals for ten hours straight once a week won't allow you to build the momentum you need for long-term success, either. Prioritization is about balance and control.

When you plan and schedule your goals, you allow yourself the time you need to focus on your top priorities. But your long-term goals are going to take time; Rome wasn't built in a day. Distractions are going to pop up continuously, and people are always going to ask for your time.

Do your best to prioritize your own goals and maintain control of your time, but don't get frustrated if life happens and you find that things keep getting in the way. Instead, continue using the tools in this chapter to help find some balance. The key is using these tools consistently.

Using These Techniques Consistently

As you begin to use these techniques, you're going to find them highly effective—I can practically guarantee it.

I can also almost guarantee (from personal experience) that when you begin to feel caught up, you're likely to abandon these tools. It's hard to take time to prioritize when you only have two or three things on your list, right?

For years, my usage of these tools would ebb and flow with how stressed and overwhelmed I would be. The more stressed I felt, the more I used the tools. Then, when I would get caught up, I would forget to apply these strategies.

But guess what—when I stopped using my prioritization and productivity tools, I would soon find myself stressed and overwhelmed all over again.

When I would reach this stressful state, I would sit down and frantically fill in my Eisenhower Matrix, start putting time blocks on my calendar, run through the Four Ds, and so on.

After I would get my head back above water, I would often wonder why I didn't continue using these strategies consistently. Perhaps it's like going to the chiropractor: I remember to go when my back hurts, but I forget to make the follow-up, preventative appointment when I'm feeling good.

My advice is to carefully craft a habit around whichever productivity strategies you decide to use and use them no matter what. Begin each day by applying these techniques, and you'll see your productivity soar and your goals realized in record time!

CHAPTER RECAP

Key Takeaways

- If you can't effectively prioritize your time or your tasks, your goals will take a back seat to the less important things that tend to pop up on a daily basis.
- It's easy to fall into the trap of becoming distracted with shallow work, empty conversations, and fruitless endeavors. When we fall into this trap, we're robbed of our productivity and focus.

These prioritization strategies can help us refocus our efforts:

- **Time Blocking** is the practice of scheduling blocks of time in advance to help complete your top priority tasks without interruption.
- Time blocks are effective, but only if you set them in advance and defend them against distraction and interruption.
- The **Four Ds** are a filter for determining the validity of a task, email, or request. The Four Ds are: Delete It, Do It, Defer It, and Delegate It.
- **Pareto's Principle** is another great filter for helping to identify which tasks or goals are most worth our time. The principle states that, for many events, roughly 80% of the effects come from 20% of the causes.
- Using Pareto's Principle, or the **80/20 rule**, we can determine which 20% of our tasks yield 80% of our results.
- The **Eisenhower Matrix** is a 2x2 grid that helps to determine the difference between Urgent and Important tasks.

- **Urgent tasks** are those that seem to scream "NOW!" and they put us in a state of reaction. These tasks often steal our time and barely move the needle on our goals.
- **Important tasks** are the ones that contribute to our long-term goals in a big way. These can be urgent, but they seldom are.
- The **ABCDE Method of Prioritization** is a filter similar to the Four Ds. The ABCDE Method helps prioritize your tasks by grading them with a letter.
- A, B, and C, are your top priorities. D-level tasks need to be delegated, E-level tasks need to be eliminated.

Memorable Quotes

- *"The key is not to prioritize what's on your schedule, but to schedule your priorities."* —Stephen Covey
- *"What is important is seldom urgent, and what is urgent is seldom important."* —Dwight D. Eisenhower

Put it into Practice

- ☐ Practice Time Blocking by scheduling out your next work week in advance. Plan one or two blocks each day for task and email management. Plan three blocks daily for your important tasks, projects, and goals.
- Clarify which of your tasks are essential to your goals using the worksheets that accompany this chapter.

The Best Tools for Tracking Your Goals

"All the tools, techniques and technology in the world are nothing without the head, heart and hands to use them wisely, kindly and mindfully."

– Rasheed Ogunlaru

Now that we have a trustworthy framework for identifying successful and exciting goals, a solid understanding of the types of goals we should be setting and strategies for prioritizing our goals, let's talk about how to keep track of our goals and our progress.

If you turn to your favorite search engine or dive into the app store on your phone, you're sure to find countless options that claim to be the best tool available for tracking goals. Maybe they are, but take it from a guy who's tried just about every gizmo that he could get his hands on: there's no one-size-fits-all tool for tracking goals.

We're all different.

Take learning styles, for example. Some of us are auditory learners, while others may be hands-on or visual learners. You can't force a hands-on learner to learn from an audio course, right?

The same is true for setting and tracking goals. Some of us are going to like analog trackers, such as notebooks and whiteboards, while others of us are going to prefer digital tools.

At the end of the day, I don't want to tell you which tools you need to be using, but I do want to highlight what I believe to be the best options. Whichever method we decide to use for tracking our goals, we need to make sure it lives up to these three guidelines:

1. You Actually Use It

This guideline may seem obvious, but many people download an app and never open it or buy an expensive journal and leave it on the shelf—a tool cannot serve you if you're not using it.

2. It Keeps You Focused

Perhaps you do use your new goal-tracker every day. That's great! But is it genuinely keeping you focused and on point?

I've seen it time and time again: people schedule goals on their calendar or write their objectives down in their notebook, but as each day zips by, they work towards everything except their goals.

Why?

Because they're not referring back to their written goals, and they succumb to the distractions of everyday life. A good tool keeps you focused.

3. It Results in Your Success

While this is possibly the most obvious of the three guidelines, it's also the most important. If whichever method of goal-tracking you're using isn't helping you succeed, it's most likely the wrong tool. Plain and simple.

Keep in Mind

As we move forward with this chapter and look at several different tools for tracking our goals, I want you to keep the three guidelines above in mind. They will serve to help you choose the best tools for your style of goal setting.

The other thing I want you to know is that, while some tools may work for several things, it's important to pick the right tool for the job at hand. For some goals, several different tracking tools might get the job done, but maybe there is a tool that works far better than the others.

Picking the Right Tool

When I was growing up, my dad worked in the construction business. He worked hard—extremely hard—on everything from small office buildings to five-year hospital jobs. And he didn't quit when he left the job site for the day. I can't tell you how many projects he built at home: shelves, sheds, cabins, furniture, his house—you name it, he's probably built it.

My favorite part of my dad's job was all of the skills he taught to me. Even to this day, the smell of sawdust, the sound of a circular saw, and the rapping of a hammer take me back to all the childhood projects we worked on together. I can't even use a tape measure without thinking back to all the neat things I watched dad build.

So why am I telling you this?

Well, as you can imagine, throughout his career, my dad used more tools than most of us know to exist. I'm sure you've heard of a level or a tape measure, but what about a plumb bob or a framing square.

Everyone knows what a saw is, but did you know that there are well over twenty types of saws? Crazy, right? Even with a large volume of options available, a skilled carpenter knows which saw is right for each task at hand. You can't use a circular saw for cutting a hole in the middle of a board and you can't use a jigsaw for cutting complex miter cuts. There's a tool for every situation. The right one will lead you to success; the wrong one will most certainly spell disaster.

Don't worry, I'm getting to the point, but I'm sure you see where I'm going with this.

There may be dozens of different tools for tracking goals, and maybe several of them will work for you, but perhaps one tool works better than the others, or maybe specific tools work best for certain types of goals. The trick is in learning which tools work best for you and in which situations.

Don't be afraid to experiment and try on a lot of different options. As you'll soon see, I resisted using a paper journal for several years before I gave in and adopted it as my preferred method of tracking my goals. I don't want you to spend years using the wrong tools; I want to give you the shortcut to success.

So without further ado, let's get into the different types of goal trackers.

Write Your Goals Down in a Journal or Planner

The Best Tools for Tracking Your Goals

As I mentioned in an earlier chapter, people who write their goals down are 42 percent more likely to achieve success. 42 percent!

That statistic is why I have journals and planners listed first. Sure, I use a journal as one of my chief tools for goal-setting success, but I remain unbiased. You can draw your own conclusions, but that stat speaks for itself.

I don't want to get too deep into psychology or neuroscience in this book, but I do want to talk about the hippocampus and how it aids in the goal setting process.

The hippocampus is the part of the brain responsible for storing memories, deciding which new information to store, and is also associated with learning. [17] One of the hippocampus's primary roles is to filter and store new information with other closely related information. Having a strong foundational knowledge in a subject area makes it easier for the hippocampus to store new data about that topic. [18]

Learning an entirely new subject, on the other hand, is more challenging. If the hippocampus cannot find similar information or relevant subject matter to the latest information coming in, it may decide not to commit the data to memory.

Repeatedly writing things down allows our brains to encode the information more effectively. Through the power of repetition, writing our goals down tells the hippocampus that our written goals are essential, and we force them into our memory.

Yes, writing your goals down makes you 42 percent more likely to achieve success, but you have to write them down regularly. You can't write them down in your notebook once and put it back on the shelf—that won't work for committing your goals to memory.

Grant Cardone recommends rewriting your entire list of goals down on a legal pad every day. [19] He does it every morning and every night. But Grant isn't the only one who recommends this strategy. Success expert and author Brian Tracy also suggests rewriting your most important goals every morning. [20]

Personally, I resisted using a notebook for years. I thought it would be too much trouble to drag a thick notebook around with me, but my longtime friend and mentor, DC, consistently advised me to do so. He has filled more journals than I can count.

After several different apps failed to help me succeed with goal-setting over the years, I reluctantly bought my first journal. At first, I would leave it on my desk and only open it during meetings to take notes, but most of the time, I wouldn't even use it for that. But DC didn't give up—he kept insisting that I keep it with me at all times.

Then one day, I stumbled onto a specific journal: Michael Hyatt's Full Focus Planner. It was more expensive, but I wanted to give it a try because it looked structured and organized, something I thought might help me follow a pattern.

I was right! Michael's planner offered me a structured and guided approach to goal-setting that my plain notebook couldn't. Instead of staring at a blank page every morning and wondering what to write, his planner helped me focus on my annual and quarterly goals as well as my weekly and daily Big Three.

Flash forward to today, and you'll see me carrying this planner with me everywhere I go. I open it every morning to review and rewrite my goals, and I identify my daily Big Three tasks. I reflect on my previous day, write down my wins, and focus on the new day ahead. It's incredible!

The Full Focus Planner has been a game changer for me and my goals, but it may not be the best planner for you.

Before becoming an annual subscriber of Michael's quarterly planner, I ventured out and tried others as well. Brendon Burchard influences a lot of my goal setting and productivity strategies, so I gave his High-Performance Planner a try. I've even tried several planners that I've purchased online, including the 90X Planner, but none of them worked for me nearly as well as the Full Focus Planner.

For one reason or another, none of these other planners kept me focused or helped me succeed like the Full Focus Planner. If there's one thing I've learned for sure, it's this: writing your goals down every day works!

I said I wouldn't push you towards one tool over another, but I highly recommend you buy a goal journal and give it a try for at least ninety days. Even though I recommend starting out with the Full Focus Planner, you can start with any planner you prefer. I don't get a commission or an affiliate check from Michael either way. (But if you're reading, Michael, call me.)

Trust me—writing your goals down daily helps embed them in your brain, keeping them ever-present and top of mind.

Download Specific Apps for Data-Driven Goals

As I mentioned earlier in this chapter, if you go searching for them, you will find countless apps for tracking goals. But as we've seen, there is tremendous power in writing your goals down daily.

Will this work with an app?

The short answer is no, at least, not in my opinion. (Unless you're using stylus-enabled device and writing your goals down that way.) Apps that simply remind you of your goals daily do not replace the power of writing them down. However, if you're a strictly digital kind of person, you might find universal goal-setting apps useful.

As I mentioned earlier, I've used various different programs and apps to monitor my progress over the years, but even with push notifications, I didn't open the program and review my goals daily. Even worse, I often forgot about the apps and my goals entirely!

However, I have found apps to be extremely useful in tracking specific, concrete, data-driven goals. For example, I used Bodyspace to track my daily lifting goals when I was shooting for the 1,250-pound club at my local gym. I was following a specific program and had to input my exact lifts, reps, and weights into the app to stay on track.

I've also used apps to track specific calorie-based diet goals and step-based fitness goals. Currently, I'm using Strava to track my weekly running goals as I train for a half marathon that is months away. This is the same app I used a few years back when I was preparing for a one hundred-mile cycling race.

I believe that apps, programs, and software have a huge purpose when it comes to goal setting, especially for the data-driven goals. Looking to drink a gallon of water every day? What about hitting a particular step count? Counting calories or trying to save a certain amount of money each day? If you look hard enough, there's practically an app for almost any goal you might have.

However, these apps do not replace using your goal journal to rewrite your top-level goals each day. If I plan to run three times per week, I write that down in my weekly planning section of my Full Focus Planner. Then I write it down as a Big-Three goal on the days I plan to complete the run. That keeps my goal top-of-mind, but Strava is where I monitor the details. How far did I run? What was my time? Was I better than last week? Those are critical metrics that support my goal and they would be far more challenging to track on paper.

At the end of the day, you need to find what works for you, because, as I've said, we're all incredibly different, and we need to find tools that match our style of goal setting.

Create an Interactive Scoreboard for Your Goals

Earlier in the chapter we learned that writing your goals down every day helps to encode them into your memory via the hippocampus. While true, this is only half of the encoding process.

The other half, you ask? Well, that comes in the form of external storage and routine review. When we write our goals down every day, we tell our hippocampus that the information is important, which allows it to begin storing the data. But early in this process, there's still a chance that we dive into our day and forget about our goals before they take hold and become hard-coded memories.

That's where whiteboards, chalkboards, or cork boards can save the day. I begin every week with a weekly review and planning session. Monday morning, I spring from my bed at 4:00 a.m., grab some coffee, and look at what I accomplished the previous week.

While spring may be a strong word for how I depart from my bed (it's more like a sluggish slide onto the floor), my Monday morning review starts with questions like these:

- ✓ Last week, did I achieve my Big Three?
- ✓ What were my biggest wins? What should I celebrate? What do I feel good about?
- ✓ What could have gone better, and how will I improve going forward?

Once I'm done with my review, I plan my upcoming week and write everything in my planner—action plan, goals, you name it. After that, I transfer my daily Big Three to my whiteboard for a constant reminder.

This process is critical to my success. Trust me; I've gone weeks where I haven't made time for this morning routine, and my momentum has suffered for it.

As I sit at my home office desk each morning, over lunch, and briefly after work, I cannot help but check in on my whiteboard.

- ✓ Did I achieve my daily Big Three?
- ✓ If not, is there time to get back on track before dinner, or should I reprioritize the rest of my week?
- ✓ What is in store for me tomorrow?

This routine may sound intense, but the fact is, setting and crushing goals isn't easy work, and if it is, you're setting your goals too low.

For me, I rarely stress about not having enough time to achieve my goals, even when I might set the bar a little too high. Instead, I view goal setting as a game that I'm excited to play, and my whiteboard is my scoreboard. It tells me when I'm winning and when I need to pick up the pace and play harder.

When I look at the board, sometimes I feel the pressure of my huge goals and think, "There's just not enough time this week." Other times, I look at it and think, "I need to add more to this, I'm way ahead—I set the bar too low."

In a way, my whiteboard is more than just a scoreboard—it's also a great accountability partner. As the days go by and tasks aren't marked out, the board tells me that I'm not playing as hard as I could be, and that I'll have to hustle hard if I'm going to win in the second half.

Perhaps you're like my wife, and you find whiteboards to be an undesirable accent to your otherwise beautifully designed office. That's okay! You can buy adorable chalkboards that may suit you better. I've also seen cork boards with ribbons for tucking papers and pictures into. You could even write your goals down on a beautiful piece of cardstock and pin it to the board. You can also find really cool looking glass boards that work just like whiteboards. They're more expensive, but they blend in with the wall more, especially if you have a uniquely colored wall or want to show off some funky wallpaper.

As with all the advice in this chapter, you should feel free to experiment and find what works for you. When I combine my whiteboard with my Full Focus Planner, I feel unstoppable. But maybe those things don't work for you. Instead, perhaps you need twenty-five Post-It Notes stuck to your computer monitor. Then as you complete tasks, you throw away a Post-It.

Whatever it is, develop a system that you enjoy. Success in goal setting comes down to daily action and progress, so find a way to track your progress and stick to it, day in and day out.

Schedules Your Priorities on Your Calendar

The last tool I want to tell you about is one you may already be using: your digital calendar. Brendon Burchard says that he can tell what a person's priorities are simply by looking at their calendar. As I mentioned in the previous chapter, I have everything on my calendar, from my morning runs and gym time to my writing blocks and family time. But what about you?

Is fitness one of your goals? Is it on your calendar?

Do you want to write a book? Is your daily writing block on your calendar?

Do you want to spend more quality time with your family? What do you have scheduled on your calendar?

As we saw in the previous chapter, time blocking is an essential strategy for achieving our goals because there are so many people, tasks, events, and so on that can slip in and consume our days if we're not intentional about how we spend our time. Time blocking is a fantastic tool, but you have to take time to get those blocks onto your calendar.

I use Microsoft Outlook, which syncs to my phone, so I set all of my time blocks, my daily Big three, and any other vital tasks on my calendar in that program. Then as I move through my day, I'm reminded of my appointments via an alert.

As a note, calendar notifications are one of the few alerts I have activated on my phone. I want to know that when my phone alerts me, it's something important and not just another Facebook update.

One of my favorite features of my digital calendar is the recurring events. If I want to write for fifty minutes every morning, I can easily add that as a recurring event. If I need to adjust it, I can do it once to update the entire chain of events. It's easy!

Best of all, you don't have to have Outlook to use any of these features. Free email clients like Gmail offer the same service, so if you haven't already, sign up for an account and start using the calendar. Oh, and be sure to sync it to your phone, too.

It may seem like overkill at first, but be sure to schedule all of your priorities. Remember, if it's truly important to you, it needs to be on your calendar with a designated time for getting it done.

Tracking Your Goals

I've said it a few times already in this chapter, but it's vital that you monitor your goals using one, some, or all of these techniques and tools. Which of them you use is entirely up to you, even if it's not one that I've covered in this book. The sky's the limit, but remember the three guidelines for choosing an effective goal-tracking tool:

1. You actually use it
2. It keeps you focused
3. It results in your success

Once you've identified your goals, start experimenting with different goal-tracking techniques, and find out what works for you.

Everything will be somewhat challenging to do consistently at first because it takes roughly sixty-six days to form a new habit, so don't give up on a tool too soon. It may feel like it's the wrong tool for you, but it could just be that it's new and you haven't formed the habit yet.

Remember, I resisted using a planner for years before deciding to stick with it. Now it's my favorite way to keep up with my goals.

CHAPTER RECAP

Key Takeaways

- With countless apps, tools, templates, and frameworks available, it's important to know that there is **no one-size-fits-all tool** for tracking goals.
- Some of us are going to like analog trackers, while others of us are going to prefer digital tools. Regardless of which tools you use to track your goals, make sure it follows these three guidelines:
  1. **You Actually Use It**
     A tool cannot serve you if you're not using it.
  2. **It Keeps You Focused**
     A good tracking tool keeps you focused and free of distractions.
  3. **It Results in Your Success**
     If whichever method of goal-tracking you're using isn't helping you succeed, it's most likely the wrong tool.
- There are countless tools for tracking goals available. **Don't be afraid to experiment** and try different tools. Perhaps one tool works better than the others. Maybe some tools work better for particular types of goals. The trick is to learn which tools work best for you and in which situations.
- **Paper Planners and Journals**
  Writing your goals down daily helps embed them in your brain, keeping them ever-present and top of mind. That's why people who write their goals down are 42% more likely to achieve success!
- **Apps and Programs**
  While apps cannot replace the power of writing your goals down daily, they are extremely useful in tracking specific, concrete, data-driven goals. For

example: tracking calories, keeping track of a weight-lifting or running program, or even how much water you consume daily.

- **Interactive Scoreboards**
  Using a whiteboard, chalkboard, or similar tool will keep your goals front and center at all times, helping to ensure your success. Use these tools to visibly plan your goals, track your progress, and cross off your wins.
- **Schedules and Calendars**
  Your calendar is a clear snapshot of your priorities and where you spend your time. Use it to carve out dedicated time for pursuing your goals.
- Success in goal setting comes down to daily action and progress, so find a way to track your progress and stick to it, day in and day out.
- It takes roughly 66 days to form a new habit, so don't give up on a new tool soon.

Put it into Practice

- ☐ Over the next several weeks or months, experiment with some or all of the goal tracking tools found in this chapter and find the ones that work best for you.
- ↪ Use the corresponding worksheets to help assess which tools work best for you.

Rapid Recap: Section 2

In this section of the book, we've covered a tremendous amount of content.

We learned a new framework by which to evaluate our goals, **The FOCUSED Framework**. This framework was designed to help you choose goals that have the highest chance for success in your life.

We also learned several universal goals that every Goal Getter should be setting: long-term goals (3-5 Years), annual and quarterly goals, action goals, and habit goals. In combination, these types of goals will help you achieve massive success in your life.

Next, we covered how to prioritize using techniques like time blocking, the Four Ds (Delete it, Do it, Defer it, and Delegate it), Pareto's Principle, aka The 80/20 Rule, The Eisenhower Matrix, and the ABCDE Method of Prioritization. Separately or in combination, these strategies will help you stay on top of your priorities and schedule so that you can focus on crushing your most significant goals.

Lastly, I provided you with several tools for tracking your goals. From classics like a journal or a whiteboard to specific, data-driven apps and digital calendars, I attempted to share with you the tools that I've seen result in the highest levels of goal-setting success. Remember, use what works for you.

I've spent a great deal of this book talking about how goals are superior to resolutions, and I stand by that. In my opinion, resolutions are doomed for failure right from the start.

With goal setting, your chances for success are vastly improved, but success still isn't guaranteed. That's why we need to establish a system for long-term success.

In the chapters ahead, we're going to learn how to build a network of support. When things get difficult, who should you call? Your accountability partner? A mentor? A mastermind group? The answers are ahead.

We're also going to learn how to sustain long-term high performance with our goal setting. Unlike with New Year's resolutions, we're in this for the long haul, and we need to be able to keep our performance up for life. We're Goal Getters; we've got this!

As we'll see in chapter 11, routines play a vital role in long-term successful goal setting. Routines can help automate some of our goal setting, allowing us to crush more goals with far less energy.

The last part of section three will demonstrate how momentum will become the driving force for your long-term success. When we set annual resolutions, we tend to start and stop, which kills our forward momentum. With goal setting, momentum is everything.

Rapid Recap

The upcoming chapters are intended to take you from setting goals to crushing goals. If you're ready, don't wait another second. Let's do this!

SECTION 3
ESTABLISHING A SYSTEM FOR SUCCESS

Assemble a Support Team

"If you want to go fast, go alone. If you want to go far, go together."

– African Proverb

When you're in the early stages of setting goals and building habits and routines, the most challenging thing can be sticking to your plan.

In the early days of my goal-setting experience, I would sit down on Monday mornings, write out my goals, and schedule time blocks for working on my top priorities. Then by Wednesday morning, I would completely fall apart.

It's true!

I would start each day with a solid plan of attack. But then I would drive into the office and allow my priorities and goals to take a back seat to anything else that came up.

That's not to say I work with a lot of overly demanding people who think their goals are more important than my own—I don't. It's just far more comfortable to go with the flow of the day than it is to swim against the current. When we take deliberate action towards our goals, we have to defend our time, reprioritize our ever-changing list of tasks, and work to stay focused on the big picture.

It's exhausting work, this game of goal-setting.

That's why building a support team is so important. A system of success can look different for everyone. For me, it's my weekly lunch-time Mastermind group. I meet with seven other guys, and we discuss our goals, talk through our hang-ups, share our plans, and keep each other accountable. It's amazingly effective and fulfilling at the same time.

I'm going to cover Mastermind groups in more detail in a minute, but maybe larger groups aren't your cup of tea. That's okay! I'm going to cover several different avenues for building your network of success, and it starts with the classic, one-on-one accountability partner.

Accountability Partners

Accountability partners are the most common method for staying committed to your goals, and the concept has probably been around since the dawn of time.

As you begin to think about looking for an accountability partner, you might wonder which traits a reliable partner might possess. It's a great question. A great accountability partner is not just someone you share your goals with before getting back to discussing the recent plots to your favorite TV shows.

To establish an effective accountability partnership, you need to consider the following three pillars: trust, respect, and a mutual understanding of the relationship

Trust

When you look for an accountability partner, you have to find someone you already trust or will be able to trust over time. You're going to be sharing your goals with this person and possibly even some of your problems. As your relationship evolves, you may even begin to share intimate details about your life—pain points, relationship problems, bad habits, and so on.

Therefore, you want to make sure that anything you discuss with this person is kept confidential. And, because an accountability partnership goes both ways, you have to be willing to extend those same courtesies to your partner as well.

Having a partner that you trust will make sharing in the process more comfortable and will allow a close bond to form. Without trust, neither of you will be able to keep each other accountable.

Respect

For an accountability partner relationship to truly work, you have to respect each other, and you have to conduct yourself respectfully.

If my accountability partner and I have a gym pact, I have to respect him enough not to leave him hanging at the gym at five in the morning. But if I do sleep in and leave him hanging, I need to respect the fact that he's going to have to call me out on it. The relationship demands that accountability, or it all falls apart.

It's not personal and it's not meant to hurt feelings, but if partners don't respect each other enough to call each other out when they fail, it can't work. It's the mutual respect and the reluctance of letting each other down that makes the relationship effective.

Mutual Understanding

An accountability partnership cannot thrive without a shared understanding of what the relationship is all about—an agreed-upon set of terms, if you will.

How will you stay in touch? Are you going to text one another in moments of weakness? Are you going to meet on a routine basis to compare progress? How will you address each other should you fail to uphold your end of the agreement?

Those are just a few of the things you and your partner need to consider and talk through, but the most critical element is this: accountability must be agreed upon.

This principle is one that took me a while to learn. My wife used to share her workout goals with me, and then I would chime in occasionally, "Hey, I thought you were going to work out today? You should really do that—it was your goal, remember?"

Bossy much?

From my experience, this approach is not a good idea. You see, my wife was simply sharing a goal with me—accountability was neither wanted nor requested. When I would attempt to provide unsolicited accountability, all she heard was criticism, and who could blame her. If accountability isn't agreed upon and you offer it up anyway, it comes across more like nagging than helpful accountability.

As you can see, there are several aspects and nuances to work through when establishing these three pillars. However, if you want your accountability partnership to be effective, you can't skip these crucial conversations.

Now, let's talk about finding an ideal accountability partner.

Picking an Ideal Partner

Okay, so maybe you have several people in your life that you trust and respect, but are they good candidates for an accountability partner?

Take my wife, for example. We love, trust, and respect one another, but we're often not ideal accountability partners for each other.

I like to get up between four and five in the morning, and she wants to sleep in as long as she can. We can't agree on a time to get up, and that's okay.

I enjoy working out; she's not a huge fan. She likes to go at her own pace and only enjoys working out when she's in the mood. That's okay, too, but it probably means we're not good accountability partners for each other when it comes to early morning workouts.

When you're looking for accountability partners, make sure that you share common goals, schedules, interests, and routines. Those things don't have to be an exact match, but some commonality will help establish a solid partnership. If your lives are too different, you may not be able to find common ground or a similar schedule which will make accountability near impossible.

For example, if I want to find an ideal accountability partner for five a.m. workouts, I need to find someone who also wants to get up early in the morning. Otherwise, I'm going to be facing an uphill battle. Not only would I be pushing this person to work out with me at five, but I'd also be struggling to help him get up early enough to do so.

When you sign up to be someone's accountability partner, you're not signing up to be a drill sergeant. The relationship is supposed to help both parties succeed; it's supposed to be supportive, not combative. If you're spending most of your energy trying to push your partner forward, then he or she isn't the right partner for you.

It's much easier to take the time to select the right accountability partner than it is to break up with them later. It may take some time, but finding the ideal partner is worth the time it takes.

Trying to use the same accountability partner for every area of your life is another common stumbling block people run into. The fact is, you may need different partners for different areas of your life. You could have a fitness partner, a career partner, and so on.

It might be difficult for your running partner to give you solid career advice if he or she has no idea what your industry looks like. It's okay to ask your running partner for career advice, but if you have specific career goals, you might want an accountability partner who understands your industry, your goals, and the challenges you might face along the way.

This relationship can look more like mentorship, but we'll get to that in a minute. First, let's talk more about Mastermind groups.

Mastermind Groups

Mastermind groups are often also referred to as accountability groups, peer groups, or even support groups. Based on the previous section, it might sound like a mastermind group is a collection of accountability partners, but that is only partially true.

Assemble a Support Team

While accountability is a part of a mastermind group's mission, it's not the core purpose. Participants of a mastermind group raise the bar by challenging each other to create and implement goals, brainstorm ideas, and support each other in all areas of life with total honesty, respect, and compassion.

As we pursue goal setting, we will begin to face new challenges and encounter new problems. As we'll see in a minute, mentors can help us overcome the specific issues that they've encountered before, but what about new and unusual problems? What about seemingly unheard-of challenges?

The mastermind group that I'm a member of is fantastic. They help me set new goals and stay accountable to those goals, but they also help me talk through my hang-ups.

Upon joining this group, I had been writing this book for what seemed like ages, but I was totally stuck. The group helped me to realize that I was splitting my focus between too many projects. We'll talk about goal competition in a later chapter, but I was experiencing a particularly bad case of competing goals.

With this new realization I froze production on the blog and the podcast at dailynewyears.com and doubled down on this book. As I'm writing this chapter, I haven't touched the blog or podcast for sixty-one days and counting, but I've made massive progress on the book.

That's just one of countless ways this amazing group of high performers has helped me recently. I can't thank them enough! Personally, I love being a part of a mastermind group, but these groups may not be for everyone.

As we saw earlier, accountability partners are one-on-one relationships with people of similar goals and interests. You can have a partner for every different goal you have. Maybe you have a dedicated running partner, someone you're reading the same books with, and someone you report your daily eating logs to, as well. The possibilities are endless!

Mastermind groups, however, are more social and group-oriented. Mine in particular started with two guys I knew and it quickly blossomed from there. We meet once a week, and the group soon grew to eight guys. We capped it at eight for the sake of keeping meetings under an hour, but as you can probably guess, it's a fairly social group.

When we meet, we discuss our commitments from the previous week, any problems we may have encountered, our progress or hang-ups, what we're reading, and anything else that may spring to mind. Towards the end, we share what we're going to do during the following week to advance our goals.

If anyone has a specific challenge that they're struggling with, we talk through it as a group and brainstorm ideas for moving passed it. The format is very flexible, but you could establish a more structured group if you wanted to.

Unless you're brand new to goal setting, mastermind groups aren't too difficult to set up or to maintain. Depending on how frequently you meet, there is a time commitment, and it's essential that you come to each meeting prepared. If you decide to become part of a group, you owe them your dedication, respect, and support.

Mastermind groups are also a great way to expand your network, but I don't suggest joining one just for this reason. The primary objective of a mastermind group is to reciprocate value and help one another achieve your biggest goals. Your primary motivation should not be to use your groupmates to gain access to their connections.

Having said that, sharing connections and making new

introductions usually occurs naturally within the group. One member may need help expanding his or her business and needs additional funding. Another member may know a local banker that would be a perfect fit and would be willing to make an introduction.

This type of naturally-occurring networking is a fantastic way to reciprocate value within the group. Everyone enters the group with their own circle of connections, opening the group up to new networks and relationships. This benefit is especially useful if you're in search of a mentor for a specific area of your life.

Mentors

So far, we've covered accountability partners and mastermind groups. Think of the people in these groups as your team. Like a sports team, you all play different positions, and you all bring a unique set of skills to the team.

With that being the case, a mentor is more like a coach. A mentor has played the game you're playing before. They've mastered the game, written the playbook, and now they're looking to pass their wisdom on to a select few individuals.

Does that sound like something you would want to get in on? I know I would!

If you want to be the best, highest-selling realtor in town, wouldn't it be nice to learn directly from one of the best realtors in your local market? If you wanted to start your own successful business, wouldn't it save you a massive amount of trouble to learn from someone who's been there and done that?

Absolutely, it would!

So how do you go about finding or connecting with your first mentor? Better yet, how do you find a find a candidate when you have no idea who to ask?

Finding Your First Mentor

The first step is to start researching and monitoring your industry on the local level. Who are the players that seem to come up over and over again in the news? Who do you repeatedly see at local chamber events? Who's blowing up on social media?

I'm not in real estate, but when I think about realtors, there are just a couple that come to mind as the top realtors in my area. They seem to be everywhere all the time; almost omnipresent. They're at every event and people always seem to be talking about them. If I wanted to be a successful realtor, I would start with them.

What are your long-term goals? Are there people in your community who have done what you're trying to do? If you're unsure, start asking around. Ask your Mastermind group if they know anyone who could help mentor you on a one-on-one basis. If so, kindly ask for an introduction.

You could also ask your boss, colleagues, parents, and your friends. If social networking sites have proven anything, it's that people tend to create an intersecting web of connections. Who knows; you could have a mentor waiting for you just three connection points away through a friend-of-a-friend.

If it's easier, publicly ask for recommendations on your LinkedIn and Facebook profiles and ask your friends to share the post with their friends. In my experience, friends are always willing and able to make recommendations on social media because it's a great way to add value to their network.

Once you identify someone in your community that you like, respect, and would like to have as a mentor, start by asking them to lunch. Over lunch, get to know him or her a little

Assemble a Support Team

better. Ask them about their life, their businesses, and their success.

Share a little about yourself as well. Tell them about your goals and aspirations. Explain your motivations for wanting to achieve success and how you admire what they've done in your shared industry.

Many times, once a prospective mentor sees your common interest and goals, they will offer up their advice, but if they don't, just ask them for their opinion. Then ask if it would be okay to reach out again in the future if you have any other questions.

Finally, pay the bill and go your separate ways. Don't ask this person to be your mentor on the spot. You wouldn't ask a person to marry you on the first date, so don't ask for a formal mentorship over the first lunch.

As time goes on, reach out to the person a time or two and then gently ask if he or she would be willing to mentor you in your area of interest. Let he or she know that you're serious about your success, and you don't want to waste their time. Make it known that you would value their time and guidance and would work hard to return the favor.

If they agree, ask about how they would like to conduct the mentorship. How long are they willing to help? Three months? A Year? Indefinitely?

How often do they want to meet and for how long? Is it okay to text and call, or should you stick to email only? Work out the logistics so that it's easier on your mentor, even if it's a little more difficult for you.

Once you nail down the logistics of the mentorship, give the relationship your best effort and try to do everything that your mentor asks you to do. You may not agree with everything your mentor says, and that's okay. However, remember that you asked them to coach you for a reason, so don't dismiss his or her ideas too quickly. Your new mentor is investing time and energy in you. This is time and energy that he could be spending on countless other things, so make it count and do your absolute best.

If a direct mentorship sounds like a bit too much for you, there is one more option that I would suggest. However, this option is last on my list for a reason: it's easier, but slightly less effective.

Social Media Communities

If you're a little shy or live in a tiny community, then mentors and mastermind groups may not be possible for you. In that case, you could turn to social media communities.

If you search Facebook and LinkedIn, you will find countless communities with specific purposes.

As I write this book, I'm in a paid, private Facebook community for writers and authors. This community is a great place to ask questions about the writing, publishing, and marketing process behind creating a best-selling book.

Sure, I could track down a best-selling author and try to ask him or her to mentor me directly, but that seems time-consuming, and frankly, very unlikely to happen. Instead, this Facebook group gives me access to nearly three thousand authors. Every day, questions and answers are flying back and forth, and new friendships are forming around common goals.

As you meet new people in these groups, accountability partnerships and mentor relationships begin to form. Social communities are a fantastic place to start building these relationships. But, because you can't grab lunch or a quick cup of coffee here and there, they rarely result in deep, personal connections. That's okay!

Perhaps a deep connection isn't all that important to you. Maybe you just want someone to connect with who can help you achieve your goals. That's okay, too! Personally, I like building deep relationships and friendships that I will be able to rely on throughout my life, but you need to do what works best for you.

If a social community sounds like it could be right for you, start looking for one or two groups to join. I'm a personal development junkie, so I've joined the groups of many of the authors I follow. Brendon Burchard, Mel Robbins, and several other authors have groups that I'm a member of.

The problem is, I'm not actively engaged in those groups. However, I'm very active in the self-publishing group because I'm actively pursuing my book writing goal.

When you look for a social community to join, try to find one that you can actively engage with daily. If you want the group to help you achieve your goals, you can't sit on the sidelines. You have to join the team, get in the game, and work towards crushing your goals. And, you can't be afraid to give back, too.

Assemble Your Team

Accountability and guidance are amazing tools. Whether you're new to goal setting or you're a longtime veteran of the game, these tools can take us to new levels in life.

One of the biggest aspects of the Goal Getter's mindset is unlimited potential. With that in mind, regardless of where you're at, I think we can all agree that we can all achieve more in our lives. As Goal Getters, our work is never done because there's always another level to reach. An accountability partner, mastermind group, mentor, or a social community can help you not only see the next level but reach it.

As you move forward with your goal-setting journey, keep in mind that you can pick more than one type of accountability. Currently, I'm relying on a mastermind group and an online community, but I could easily roll an accountability partner or a mentor into the mix.

It doesn't matter what your network of success looks like. The most important thing is that you have one in place. No matter who you are or where you're at in life, there are always people ahead of you, and there's people behind you.

As you seek to improve your life and crush your goals by leaning on those ahead of you, don't forget to also reach back and help someone else along the way.

You can be someone else's mentor or accountability partner. You can help someone else build their network of success, and who knows, someday you might be someone's mentor.

Building a network of people who are going to help you achieve your goals is just one way to ensure your success over the long haul. In the next chapter, we're going to look at how we can become lifetime Goal Getters by using the Four Cs of High Performance.

Assemble a Support Team

CHAPTER RECAP

Key Takeaways

- ⊘ Goal setting is hard work, that's why building a support team is so important, especially in the beginning.
- ⊘ **Accountability Partners** are people who have similar goals and who work together to achieve those goals.
- ⊘ To establish an effective accountability partnership, you need to build your relationship on **trust, respect, and a mutual understanding of the relationship.**
- ⊘ When you're looking for accountability partners, make sure that you share **common goals, schedules, interests, and routines.**
- ⊘ You may need different accountability partners for the different areas of your life. You could have a fitness partner, a career partner, and so on.
- ⊘ Participants of a **Mastermind Group** are more than just accountability partners; they raise the bar by challenging each other to set goals, brainstorm ideas, and support each other in all areas of life with total honesty, respect, and compassion.
- ⊘ The primary objective of a mastermind group is to reciprocate value and help one another achieve your biggest goals.
- ⊘ If Accountability Partners and Mastermind Groups are your teammates, then a **Mentor** is your coach. Good mentors have mastered the game, written the playbook, and they're willing to coach up-and-comers.
- ⊘ Mentors are highly valuable because they invest time and energy in you and help you shortcut your

Assemble a Support Team

success. This is time and energy that he or she could be spending on countless other things, so make it count and do your absolute best.

- ✓ **Social Media Communities** are a fantastic solution for anyone with limited access to other high-performing individuals.
- ✓ If you have trouble finding a mentor, mastermind group, or accountability partner, seek a social community centered around your goals or area of desired growth. No matter what you're looking to achieve, there's most likely a group for it.
- ✓ Social Media Communities are great, but you have to engage and reciprocate value.
- ✓ Remember, forming these relationships takes commitment on both sides. Don't start something you don't plan to see through.

Put it into Practice

- ☐ Reach out to friends, family, colleagues, and your social networks to start looking for accountability partners and mentors. If you're ambitious, form a small mastermind group.
- ↪ Use the corresponding worksheets to help identify potential accountability partners, find your first mentor, and more!

The Four Cs of High-Performance Goal Setting

"If we practice being spectacular long enough, spectacular will become our way of being."
– Robin Sharma

As we continue talking about how to set up a system for goal-setting success, I want to address the myth of "The Overnight Success."

I feel like every time I turn around, there's someone new who seems to have made a sudden meteoric rise to success. If you look closely, you'll see this on social media, the news, and in so many other places. As a society, we've come to call these people overnight successes.

Before we go any further, I want to tell you that, just like BigFoot, there is no such thing as an overnight success. [1] Sure,

---

1 My wife and I constantly argue about the possibility of BigFoot's existence. I'm a hard no. She's a true believer.

someone might get lucky with a sudden cryptocurrency boom or stumble onto a once-in-a-lifetime deal that makes them millions of dollars, but these types of things do not point to repeatable, long-term success.

True long-term success takes time, especially with goal setting. When we compare our own journeys with these supposed overnight successes, we can quickly become discouraged. We can't help but wonder things like, "How did they achieve that so quickly and why can't I do the same?" In reality, we don't see how many years or decades these overnight successes put in before they landed on our radars.

Genuinely successful people become successful through years and years of focus, hard work, and perseverance. You might call these people high performers. They've maintained a high, steady output of effort for years. As their success begins to grow over time, it begins to compound. And then suddenly, they explode to the top, and we all see what we believe to be an overnight success. In reality, we're seeing the product of long-term high performance.

I've made this point several times throughout this book, but I want to mention it at least one more time: as you seek to set and crush the goals that will lead to your dream life, you have to focus on the longterm.

As we've seen, New Year's resolutions tend to fail due to short-term thinking. If we want to succeed in seeing our dreams come true, we have to be in it for the long haul—we have to focus on high performance.

What is High Performance?

What comes to mind when you think of high performance?

Do you think of a Navy Seal passing the rigors of BUD/S training? Perhaps you think of the cyclists climbing the long,

The Four Cs of High Performance Goal Setting

steep mountains in the Tour de France? What about the brave people who manage to ascend Everest?

I tend to think of high performance in a physical sense, and while those examples definitely apply, I want to shine the light on a broader category of people: those who set significant goals for themselves and pursue them with relentless passion, energy, and focus.

High performers are a group of people who don't quit until they've achieved the success they've been aiming for, no matter how difficult the road or how long the journey.

While a healthy, fine-tuned physique is vital for peak performance in athletes, high performance in goal setting stems from the mind. In chapter one, we examined the Goal Getter's mindset. In that chapter, I illustrated the idea that people who want to become Better Every Day never trade short-term satisfaction for long-term success. Essentially, what we're talking about there is high performance.

High performance is the key to sustained, long-term success, especially in goal setting. If you chase your goals too hard and burnout or regularly find yourself running around in circles without focus, you're not going to be able to achieve your long-term goals.

Again, I believe the lack of long-term thinking is why New Year's resolutions are so popular; they're easy to set, but I also think it's why they so often fail. It's easy to pick an arbitrary goal from thin air and work towards it for a couple of weeks, but is that strategy going to lead to your five-year dream? Not a chance!

Instead, we need to develop a system for sustained success; something that's going to take us from where we are, to where we want to go and keep us performing at optimal levels.

In Brian Tracy's book *Goals!* he outlines his three keys to peak performance: commitment, completion, and closure.

Not to steal Brian's concepts, but they're incredibly effective, and I want to highlight them in this chapter. However, I felt there was a critical element missing from his formula: competition. As you'll see in a second, competition among your goals could be the very thing robbing you of your highest performance.

So without further ado, let's take a look at the Four Cs of High Performance Goal Setting: Competition, Commitment, Completion, and Closure. [21]

Competition

The first C is competition, but not the type of competition might be thinking about.

Psychologists have a concept they refer to as "goal competition," which states that one of the most significant barriers to achieving your goals is the other goals you have. In other words, your goals are all competing against one another for your time.

Have you ever noticed how busy everyone seems to be these days? We all have a thousand things to do!

Whenever you decide to pursue a new goal, you inevitably take time away from the other goals you've been pursuing. Each goal takes time, energy, and focus, all of which are finite resources.

So how do we decide which goals to pursue? How do we keep from spinning our wheels and running around in circles for the next five years? How do we shift into high performance?

Most of us start by choosing which goals we are going to pursue. For example: "This quarter, I'm going to run a half-

The Four Cs of High Performance Goal Setting

marathon, finish my book, build a deck, and read three books." Then, for many of us, when something new and exciting comes along, we add that to the list as well. In our excitement, many of us even start on the new goal right away instead of logging it away for a better time.

"Learn how to play golf? Absolutely! I've always wanted to learn how to play! This weekend? No, I'm not busy. The deck project can wait. Let's do it!"

While oddly specific, does this situation sound familiar to you at all? How often do new and exciting opportunities pop up and find the fast track to the top of your list?

And this isn't even taking into account the goals we elect subconsciously or the goals placed upon us by our family, friends, bosses, and co-workers, etc.

All of the extra work assignments you volunteer for, the unplanned projects at home, the extracurricular activities you sign up for at your kid's school—they're all goals, and they're all competing for your time and energy.

How many goals do you have right now that you're not even counting among your core goals? Think deeply. Did you commit to a new task at work without thinking about it? Do you have to get that report or presentation completed by Friday for your boss? Yep, that's a goal, and it's competing against your other goals.

Even while writing this chapter, I can think of several goals I'm pursuing that are not in my quarterly goal planner. These necessary but unwritten goals are competing against my official goals, or at the very least, causing me to question which goals are my real goals.

It's situations like these that lead to so many of us having countless, partially completed goals competing for our time, causing stress and feelings of being overwhelmed, fatigued, and discouraged.

Dependable high performance in goal setting starts with understanding goal competition and choosing which goals not to pursue.

That's right!

Out of the twenty-five things you want to do, which five goals are you going to focus on in the coming months? More importantly, which twenty are you not going to pursue?

If you want to sustain high performance with your goals for the long haul, it's far more important to decide on the things that you're not going to attempt. Put another way, which goals are you going to intentionally save for later?

Just like with your active goals, you also need to write down your inactive, future goals so that you don't forget about them. Instead of actively pursuing them right now, write them down and store them away for a later date. You can call this your backlog of goals.

As time goes on and you think of new and exciting things to pursue, instead of jumping on them right away, which will derail all of your other goals, add them to your backlog instead. Once you've achieved some of your priority goals, you can revisit and reprioritize your backlog before committing to some new active goals.

Commitment

The second C for sustaining high-performance goal setting is commitment.

To achieve our long-term, five-year goals and the smaller goals leading up to our five-year vision, we have to truly commit to our goals. We cannot pursue them half-heartedly, and we must avoid goal competition.

When we commit to our goals, we pursue them with determination, focus, and a zero-tolerance policy for excuses. One definition of commitment is "the state of being dedicated to a cause, or activity." A far stronger definition is "an engagement or obligation that restricts freedom of action."

When you set a goal, which definition do you tend to follow? Are you dedicated, or are you so dedicated that you don't allow yourself to lose focus no matter what? That second definition seems harsh, but when we restrict our own freedom, we lock ourselves into the goals we've committed to, and we don't allow ourselves to pursue activities that are going to derail our goals.

"I can't go out tonight because I have to get up early to train for a race in the morning."

"I can't join your board of directors right now because I'm starting my first business, and I don't have any extra time."

"I can't help you with your project because I have an important project of my own."

These statements may seem selfish at first glance, but a real commitment to our goals means restricting ourselves from taking on too many other commitments. When we commit to too many things, we're guaranteed to miss the mark somewhere; you're either going to let someone else down or fail to achieve your own goals.

We can't achieve high performance in goal setting if we're not genuinely committed to our goals and the effort that it will take to reach those goals.

That's right—in addition to committing to our goals themselves, we must also commit to the effort and time they're going to take. Life-changing goals are going to be challenging. If they weren't, they wouldn't be life changing.

Writing this book is going to have a massive impact on my life, but I had to commit to hundreds of hours of writing and rewriting. I had to commit to countless four a.m. mornings. I had to put my blog and podcast on hold, two things I very much love to work on each week. I decided to unplug and hide my Xbox. I had to restrict my freedoms and actions in order to achieve my goal. I had to be fully committed to my book.

We can't always predict or plan for every challenge we might encounter while pursuing a goal, but real commitment means working towards a goal until it's 100 percent complete, regardless of the difficulties you might face along the way.

Completion

Completion may seem like an obvious variable in the high-performance, goal-setting formula, but it seems the two most challenging aspects of goal setting are getting started and achieving full completion.

Only 20 percent of people bother to set goals for themselves regularly. Of the 20 percent who do set goals, only 30 percent tend to achieve the success that they're looking for. [22]

These stats mean that only 6 percent, or 3 out of every 50 people, see success in goal setting.

Why are there so few people achieving goals?

I believe it's because there is a massive difference between doing 95 percent of a task or a goal and seeing it through to 100 percent completion.

Surprising as it may be, it's very common for people to get 90 to 95 percent of a task done and then quit altogether. Take a second to think about that. How many things have you gotten close to completing and fizzled out on or said "good enough"?

Trust me; I've not innocent here either. We've all done this, but the effects are detrimental to our future successes. To explain why this is so detrimental we have to get a little scientific.

Endorphins: The Goal-Setting Fuel

When we quit before completing a task, we never receive the endorphin release that gives us the feeling of success, accomplishment, and reward.

Endorphins are the hormones that give us a sense of well-being and elation—they're the hormones that make hard work and dedication worth the effort in the end. If we never see a goal through to completion, we never get to feel the sense of gratification that comes from these endorphins. "Even if we get 99 percent done," you ask.

Nope! No endorphins for you.

Why would we work hard towards a goal if we don't associate goal setting with pleasure?

If we always quit at the 95 percent mark, we learn to associate goal setting with hard work, but not happiness or pleasure. We've put 95 percent of the effort, but we've received 0 percent of the rewards that should come with that effort.

On the other hand, when we complete a task or see a goal through to the 100 percent mark, we receive a surge of endorphins—the bigger the task, the bigger the surge. These endorphins make us feel good about ourselves and ultimately make us want to repeat the feeling by achieving our next goal.

If we're going to be setting long-term, five-year goals for ourselves, we can't approach it with the 95 percent, goodenough mentality. We have to commit, achieve our goals, rack up some wins, and learn to associate goal setting with feelings of pleasure and success.

As we achieve more and more of our goals through this compounding effect, we will learn to love the feeling that success brings, and we'll eventually build a habit of achieving our goals. Eventually, it will seem like success is nearly automatic. You set a goal, and you achieve it. Over and over, success after success, and all because you habitually complete your goals.

So far, we've talked about avoiding goal competition, committing to our goals, and seeing them through to completion and that brings us to the fourth and final C: closure.

Closure

Before we dive in too deep, let's take a look at what closure is. How is it different from completion? Closure is the sense of resolution or conclusion. You can experience the end of something but not receive closure. Have you ever had a favorite TV show get canceled abruptly? "How was it supposed to end? What happened to the characters? Can't we get one more episode to close things out?"

When this happens, we fail to receive closure. Sure, the show is over; it's complete in the eyes of the production company, but there was no conclusion, no closure.

Finding closure in the goals we've completed is easy. We achieve our goal, get a surge of endorphins, and celebrate our success. We check the goal off on our to-do list, and we move onto our next exciting goal.

But what about the goals we don't achieve? Nothing causes more stress and feelings of being overwhelmed and dissatisfied than unfinished business.

We all have goals we're working hard to see realized. We pour our passion and energy into these goals, and when they're complete, we feel amazing. But when we abandon or lose track of a goal due to the lack of focus, we leave behind what I call "energy anchors."

Forgotten Goals and Energy Anchors

Energy anchors pull at us from behind, draining our energy and our momentum.

When we lose track of a goal, our subconscious mind tries to remind us of what we've forgotten. And, if we give up on a goal prematurely, our brain is still going to warn us about it over and over continually.

These situations lead to an ever-growing sense of stress. You know the nagging feeling—the one that keeps making you feel like you've forgotten something even though you can't remember what it is. Then at two in the morning, you wake up thinking about a goal you forgot, or it suddenly springs to mind during a meeting or while you're in the shower.

It can be maddening!

Multiply that feeling by the number of unfinished things you've left in your wake, and you might break out into a cold sweat.

But as we've seen, sometimes we have to decide not to pursue a goal—sometimes our priorities change. How can we get closure on a goal that we're choosing to leave behind on purpose?

How can we eliminate some of these energy anchors going forward?

Determine Why You're Abandoning a Goal

I often talk about connecting your goals with a strong *why* for achieving maximum success, but you also need to look at why you quit, paused, or postponed a goal.

Sometimes, the timing isn't right, so we have to postpone a goal or put it in our backlog for a later date.

If that's the case, that's okay, but you need to acknowledge that truth. Tell yourself that the timing isn't right and write the goal on your backlog. This way it will be out of your mind, but you won't feel like you've abandoned the goal.

For a long time, I was trying to write this book while maintaining the blog and podcast. Creating content for all three was draining, so I would often skip out on writing the book, but it was always there; it had become an energy anchor. I kept feeling like I had this massive goal that I was making zero progress towards achieving.

Finally, I decided that the book was more important than the blog, at least for now. I told myself that it would be okay to pause the blog and podcast in order to work on the book. In doing so, I freed my mind to focus on the book without distraction and stress.

If it's not the timing or prioritization that's wrong, but the goal itself is wrong, then think about why the goal is wrong for you. You need to dig deep and explore the why in great detail.

If you're quitting the goal because it became difficult or lost its luster, then you're most likely creating an energy anchor that will continue to haunt you. You'll always wonder what-if.

However, if the goal is wrong because of a legitimate reason, identify that reason and connect with it. Permit yourself to set a new goal that's more significant to you.

It's easy to set goals for the wrong reasons, whether it be fear of missing out (FOMO) or jumping on the wrong bandwagon, but you shouldn't feel bad about ditching the goals that are wrong for you. If you continue to pursue them even when you don't want to, you're going to become exhausted and probably fail. If you abandon the goal with no thought as to why then you're also going to feel like you've failed.

But if you connect with why you're changing direction and ensure that your reasoning is founded in truth and not in excuses, then you'll get the closure you need to keep moving forward with energy and passion.

Putting the Four Cs Into Practice

As you near the end of this chapter, you might be wondering where to start with the Four Cs. Truthfully, it all depends on where you're at in your goal-setting journey.

If you've never set goals before, revisit chapter 6 and explore the various types of goals you can set and write all of your goals down. Next, prioritize those goals and be sure to avoid goal competition.

If you've already been setting goals, but you're struggling, sit down and evaluate everything you've been doing, everything you've wanted to do, and everything you have done. Start by celebrating your wins. Where have you succeeded? What have you accomplished?

Then decide on which goals you're going to focus on and which ones you're not. For the ones you're not going to pursue, give yourself permission to leave them behind and get the closure you need. Cut ties with those energy anchors.

Finally, commit to the goals you're setting for yourself and see them through to completion before setting or pursuing any new goals. As new and exciting goals come along, place them on your backlog for a later date.

Practice Makes Perfect

As with all things, practice makes perfect. If at first, you don't succeed, try again. Don't give in to frustration or feelings of failure. Remember, you've only failed if you've quit trying.

If you set a goal and find yourself wanting to quit, think about why and get closure if you can. If you can't find closure because you're only finding excuses to quit, keep pushing. Don't quit just because things get hard! Connect with why you set that goal in the first place, tie it to a deeper meaning, and press forward.

And when you complete a goal, be careful not to move on too quickly. Allow yourself to feel the win and celebrate your success.

Over time, these practices will become second nature, but in the meantime, remember your goal planner and don't forget to check in with that daily.

Now that we have a solid understanding of Four Cs of high-performance goal setting and we've assembled a support team, we're well on our way towards building our system of success.

Our support team will provide us long-term accountability and guidance and the Four Cs will allow us to better evaluate our goals. Are our goals competing against one another? Did we quit because things got hard, or was the goal all wrong? We can also reduce energy anchors by finding either closure or completion with our goals.

Still ahead, we have two more tools for helping to crush our goals for the rest of our lives. The first is building a daily, success-driven routine. Routines are powerful, and if used correctly, can help to automate some of our goals by building them into our daily lives.

Better yet, great routines can help us build massive momentum with our goals, allowing us to compound our success over time.

CHAPTER RECAP

Key Takeaways

- There is no such thing as an overnight success.
- Genuinely successful people become successful through years and years of focus, hard work, and perseverance. These people are high performers.
- As you seek to set and crush the goals that will lead to your dream life, you have to focus on long-term, high-performance goal setting.
- **Goal Competition** states that one of the most significant barriers to achieving your goals is the other goals you have. The goals you elect to postpone or disregard are potentially more important than the goals you choose to pursue.
- Out of the twenty-five things you want to do, which five goals are you going to focus on in the coming months? More importantly, which twenty are you not going to pursue? Be sure to keep track of your active goals and your backlog goals.
- **Commitment** to your goals means that you pursue them with determination, focus, and a zero-tolerance policy for excuses.
- **Commitment has two definitions:**

    1. "The state of being dedicated to a cause, or activity."

    2. "An engagement or obligation that restricts freedom of action."

    When you set a goal, which definition do you tend to follow? Are you dedicated, or are you so dedicated that you don't allow yourself to quit?

- We can't achieve high performance in goal setting if we're not genuinely committed to our goals AND

- the effort that it will take to reach those goals.
- **Completion** means seeing a goal through and finishing it 100 percent. 90-95 percent doesn't count!
- Seeing a goal through to 100 percent completion provides a surge of **Endorphins** that serve as a reward for a job well done. Seeing a goal through to 95 percent equates 95 percent of the work with 0 percent of the reward.
- **Closure** is a sense of resolution or conclusion. We receive closure when we achieve a goal and celebrate our success before moving on.
- When we abandon a goal without closure, we create stressful **Energy Anchors** that drain us of our future high performance and success.
- To avoid creating Energy Anchors, ensure that your reasons for abandoning your goal are founded in truth and not in excuses. Don't quit because things get hard, but don't forcefully pursue a goal that you no longer wish to achieve. Either way, find closure before moving on.

Put it into Practice

The corresponding worksheets will guide you through the process of using the Four Cs to assess your past, current, and future goals. Use them to provide yourself with a clean slate.

Develop a Daily, Success-Driven Routine

> *"You will never change your life until you change something you do daily. The secret of your success is found in your daily routine."*
>
> – John C. Maxwell

When it comes to success, there's no reason to reinvent the wheel, right?

One of the things I enjoy is analyzing successful people and studying their strategies so that I can explore what works best for myself. And as I explore the world of personal development, I love to share my findings on my blog.

Since starting Daily New Year's, I've noticed several recurring trends emerging in what I write about. One of the most prominent trends is that people who achieve higher levels of success do so by developing a powerful daily routine built on positive habits.

On the blog, I've written about how routines have helped me

overcome obstacles, how routines can help build strong habits, and how you can craft a routine around achieving your goals. Routines can even help you achieve several goals at once.

What can I say? I guess I love routines!

So as we explore methods for building a goal-setting system, I want to explain why routines are so crucial to successful goal setting. I also want to talk about how positive habits play a significant role in building a daily routine and how to establish a new daily routine that works for both you and your goals.

What is a Daily Routine?

Let's start by defining a routine. There are several official definitions out there, but none that I liked enough for this chapter, so I wrote a custom definition for this book: A routine is a habitual performance of an established set of actions to the near point of automation.

Let's look at this a little closer, shall we? When was the last time you had to think about your morning routine for getting ready for work? Most people follow the same steps in the same order every day. Snooze the alarm a time or two, roll out of bed, brush your teeth, take a shower, put on your clothes, and so on.

At most, you might have to decide which outfit to wear, but I'd wager that the process you follow each morning is nearly automatic at this point. Your morning routine is a habitual performance of an established set of actions to the near point of automation, right?

You don't have to think about it—it just happens. How do you think it got that way?

Obviously, we're not going to spend two hours getting ready

for work if we can sleep longer and get ready in fifteen minutes. Without even realizing it, we gravitate towards the most efficient process through subconscious trial and error.

If we can build an efficient daily routine for getting ready for work, would you agree that it's possible to create new routines in other areas of our lives as well?

I hope you said yes because I'm about to make a strong case for how we can build routines around our goals, but first, I want to address a potentially negative side to routines: can they limit and stagnate our lives?

Can Routines Limit Our Lives?

Before we get into why routines are so crucial to success, I want to address another side of the argument. Some people will argue that routines hold us back from life or will reduce our spontaneity and sense of adventure.

To those of you who see this side of routines, I want to say that I agree with you, to an extent.

Yes, I will concede that if you always eat the same foods, watch the same shows over and over, go on the same vacations, frequent the same restaurants, play the same games, exhaust the same hobbies, and so on, you might be missing out on all that life has to offer.

If that is how you see routines, then I would have no choice but to agree with you, but the point of this chapter is not to convince you to automate and roboticize your entire life. Not at all!

To live life to the fullest, we have to experience new things and seek out new adventures. I never knew that I would love scuba diving so much until I tried it a few years ago, and now it's one of my favorite things to do. So please, go on some adventures. Try new foods. Do things that excite you.

The point of this chapter is to illustrate how daily routines can help us achieve success with our goals. Remember, in this section of the book, we're learning how to build a system of success around our goals and routines are a great way to help ensure that success.

If I've managed to bring you around to seeing how routines can work in your favor without limiting your sense of adventure, let's take a look at exactly how routines work to support your goals.

The Three Energy Multipliers

Routines are powerful for many reasons. Sure, they can help us get ready for work in fifteen minutes, but that's not all they can do. At a higher level, routines can support our goals by reducing decision fatigue, conserving willpower, and allowing us to build momentum, all of which multiply our energy and boost our success.

Routines Reduce Decision Fatigue

Do you ever get tired of making decisions? Because I know I do! What am I going to wear today? What am I going to have for breakfast/lunch/dinner? Which task should I do first? Which goal is most important today?

The list goes on and on as options come at us from every angle. It can be challenging to prioritize everything you have to do every day. That's why people like Steve Jobs and Mark Zuckerberg have been known to wear the same outfits every day—it's one less decision to make!

Having a daily routine can help reduce decision fatigue by allowing us to automate some of our decisions.

I wrote about this extensively on the blog, but in 2015, I built a routine around my goal to get into the 1,250-pound club at my local gym. I would get up every day at 4:45, go to the gym, follow my power-lifting program, and drink a massive protein shake. I did this every day without fail, and all before going into the office.

Before I converted this series of actions into a daily routine, the decision to get up at 4:45 every day was an exhausting, internal battle that taxed my decision-making ability, and pushing myself to the gym would drain my decision-making ability even further.

"Should I sleep In?"

"Can I make this up tomorrow?"

"Maybe I can squeeze in a lift at lunch?"

All decisions.

As the day wore on, each decision would become more difficult. Eventually, I would reach a point where I would start making poor decisions such as eating take-out or fast food for dinner as opposed to planning out a healthy meal with my wife.

However, as I continued to build the routine, waking up early and going to the gym became nearly automatic. After a while, I could jump out of bed at 4:45 and zip over to the gym without a second thought, leaving my decision-making ability intact for the day to come.

It's nearly impossible to account for every decision we make all day long. From traffic decisions you make in the car, deciding which emails you respond to, and whether or not to take a call or let it go to voicemail, we make thousands of subconscious decisions every day.

Have you ever noticed that some days seem significantly more draining than others, even though the work you've done was pretty standard? I've heard the phrase, "I don't know why I'm so tired today" countless times. Decisions don't seem like work because, for the most part, we're not even aware that we're making so many.

When we save our goals for the end of the day, we risk running out of energy and decision-making power, leaving our goals unfulfilled. On the other hand, when we build routines around our goals, we ensure our success by cutting out decisions and hardwiring our goals into our daily routine.

Routines Conserve Willpower

Much like decision making, we have a limited amount of willpower and motivation each day. When we use it all up on trivial things, there is little willpower left to achieve what matters.

Remember my morning routine for going to the gym? At first, deciding to do that everyday taxed my decision-making ability, but worse, it practically tanked my willpower. In the early days of building that routine, I had to use most of my daily willpower for following through with my goal.

Now there's not a gauge for measuring willpower, but when we actively push ourselves towards a goal, or we actively resist a temptation, the willpower meter is running.

For example, if you're trying to eat healthily and lose weight, but someone brings donuts into the office, you start having that internal debate, right? "You're trying to lose weight; you don't need that donut. But one won't hurt, right? No, you don't need it. You were doing so good."

Trust me; I've had this argument with myself more than a few times.

Again, I don't mean to pick on weight loss, but I think it's an example most of us can relate to, and every time you engage in such an argument, you're depleting your willpower.

> *"Get out of bed; you need to go to the gym if you're going to get in shape. But the bed feels so good, and I'm tired. I could always make it up tomorrow. No, you said that last week, too. Get up!"*

Willpower draining.

But here's the good news—just like with decision making, routines can help us to automate our goals, reduce decisions, and leave more of our willpower intact. However, it takes time. In the early phases of building routines, you're always going to have to get over the initial, willpower-draining hump, but if you stick with it, you'll be building momentum and crushing your goals in no time.

Routines Build Momentum

If I've said it once, I've said it a thousand times: Starting small, taking action, and building momentum are the keys to success in any endeavor.

Do you agree? I've written about taking action and building momentum several times on my blog before, but I'll give you the SparkNotes version here.

Starting something new isn't very impactful if you keep quitting. Think about a rocket aiming for the moon. What if that rocket launched, burned up most of its fuel, only to return to Earth before escaping the atmosphere? Then what if it repeatedly refueled, relaunched, and landed again before clearing the atmosphere. It wouldn't make much sense, right? It would be terribly inefficient, not to mention a significant waste of time and energy.

Starting and stopping over and over again in your life is just like that rocket wasting fuel.

Building momentum, however, is like breaking free of the atmosphere and reaching space. Once there, the zero gravity keeps the rocket afloat, allowing the pilot to use relatively small amounts of fuel to propel and steer the rocket through space.

I recently read an article from The Huffington Post, and it said,

> "In the 1967 Apollo mission to the moon, the Saturn V rockets needed over 500,000 gallons of fuel just to break free of the Earth's atmosphere. The final stage of the trip only required 86,059 gallons of fuel. That means it took nearly 5.8 times as much effort to launch as it did to keep the momentum." [23]

Are you picking up what I'm putting down?

When we build strong routines, we reduce the number of decisions we have to make, we conserve our willpower, and we build massive momentum towards our goals!

Successful people understand how to use daily routines to their advantage. They automate the mundane or repetitive tasks in their lives so that they can focus on their long-term goals instead.

At this point, I trust you're seeing the vital role that routines play in building a system of success around our goals. A little later in the chapter, I'm going to show you how to start building these routines, but before I do, I want to explain the connection between habits and routines.

The Routine/Habit Connection

I recently listened to *The Power of Habit: Why We Do What We Do in Life and Business* by Charles Duhigg on Audible, and it's fascinating how much impact habits have on our lives, even if we don't realize it.

In the book, he talks about a medical patient named Eugene Pauly, who suffered damage to his medial temporal lobe, the area of the brain responsible for memory. Even though Eugene's medial temporal lobe was severely damaged and he couldn't remember new information for more than a minute or two at a time, he was still able to follow habit-based routines that were established far earlier in his life.

Personally, I find this absolutely remarkable.

Duhigg's book covers this in far more detail, but the primary discovery that doctors and scientists made was that habits are stored separately from our memories. Similar to a computer, our brain works to store information in the most efficient and useful way possible. Memories are stored on the hard drive while our habits and routines are stored in the operating system.

Because we receive so much new information every day, our brains store habits in an effort to reduce overall processing power.

Let's take driving, for example. Imagine how hard it would be to learn new things if we had to consciously remember how to drive every day. Have you ever noticed how it gets easier to back the car out of the driveway the more times you do it? That's a stored habit at work!

The first time you do it, you must account for dozens of variables: when to accelerate, brake, or use the mirror, how much to turn the wheels, how to avoid the obstacles in your driveway, and to check for traffic. There's a great deal of thinking that goes on the first few times you back out of the drive, but after a while, the habit becomes a subroutine in your mind and autopilot takes over.

Habits are how the brain learns to do things without constant deliberation, so instead of thinking about how to back out of the driveway, you can focus on the bigger picture.

So how can you use this fantastic discovery to your advantage? It's simple, really; you can work to build routines that support and automate your goals. For you, it may not be waking up at 4:45 in the morning to lift weights, but you can use the power of routines to achieve nearly any goal you can imagine.

How to Establish a New Routine

We've covered a great deal of information in this chapter, and by now you've seen how useful routines can be. But habits and routines are difficult to build, so how do we set them up so that they stand the test of time?

If you want to read one book per month, you could start a daily routine to read a predetermined number of pages during your lunch break or before bed. If you're going to run a half-marathon, you could start a daily routine for running before work. If your goal was to write a book, you could establish a three-hour, four a.m. writing routine like the one I used to write this book.

Those examples are specific to me and, to be honest, they're pretty simplistic. Maybe you want to open a bakery or perhaps you want to get your master's in business administration. How can you build a routine to achieve something more complicated?

If you want to build a robust and success-driven routine that

Develop a Daily, Success-Driven Routine

will help to crush your long-term goals, follow these four steps:

1. Identify Your Long-Term Goals

Before we begin crafting a daily routine to help streamline our success, we need to look at what we're hoping to achieve. What are your five, ten, fifteen, and twenty-year goals?

I know what you're thinking; it can be daunting to think about the future, especially twenty years from now. Will our daily habits and routines really impact our lives twenty years from now? The short answer is yes!

I think we can agree that we're all going to end up somewhere in life. As life moves forward, so do we. We can either choose a destination and make travel plans that will take us there (our goals and routines), or we can drift through life and hope that we've ended up somewhere we like in the end.

In other words, we need to begin with the end in mind.

When you begin to build a daily routine, it needs to help move you closer to the dream you have for your future. Even though it may be difficult to project your life forward five to ten years, it's essential that you do so before thinking about establishing your routines.

If you're unsure of where you want your life to go, refer back to the Blue-Sky Thinking section of chapter six. It will help you identify your long-term goals and the dream life that you want for yourself.

2. Break Your Goals Down

The next critical step in building a successful daily routine is to break your long-term goals into manageable milestones and daily activities.

Two of my larger goals are to write a personal development book on the topic of goal setting (you're seeing that goal realized right now) and to speak on a stage to a massive audience at the Global Leadership Summit or a similar event.

To move closer to those goals, I need to break things down into manageable pieces. For this book, it was early morning writing sessions every day at four a.m. After the first draft, I would use that time for editing, crafting worksheets, laying out pages, and so on.

For speaking on a stage to ten thousand people, the routine I build may not be in the form of daily actions. I need to hone my speaking skills and pick up some experience. For that, I might join ToastMasters and work towards improving my skills in a weekly group meeting. From there, I might spend one or two hours per week looking for and applying to speaking engagements at Chamber events, high schools, non-profits, or local businesses.

To achieve my speaking goal, I can't hope to wake up as a great speaker one day; I need to rack up hundreds of small wins and build on my success.

You need to do the same thing with your goals.

To do so, spend some time and break your long-term goals down into monthly, weekly, and daily actions. The more you can break your goals down, the easier it will be to establish a daily routine. This process is very similar to those found in chapter 6, but this time we're focused on breaking things down to benefit our routines.

3. Build a Daily Routine Around Your Goals

Once you've broken your goals down into manageable pieces,

Develop a Daily, Success-Driven Routine

begin looking for ways to combine your actions into a routine. As I mentioned, for my book, that was a daily three-hour writing block, but not all routines are made up of repetitive daily actions.

For example, to consistently release weekly blog posts and episodes of the Daily New Year's Podcast, I have a daily routine to move the needle on my goals. I use time blocking to carve out time every day for research, writing, editing, designing, generating social content, and promoting my articles. No two days look the same, but my daily routine supports my weekly goal.

Here's another example. If you want to open a bakery, you won't get there by baking for an hour every day. Yes, you have to hone your baking skills, but you also have to find a location for your shop, set up your business, acquire financing, order equipment, build a brand, and so on.

To see this goal realized, you would have to accomplish hundreds of different tasks. You can still build a daily routine around this goal by setting aside time to work towards your goal every day.

Regardless of my current goals, waking up at four a.m. has been a game-changing routine. No matter what I'm focusing on, the three-hour window I have before my official workday begins has been vital to my success. It's fifteen hours per week that I get to focus on my goals.

That three-hour window may look different month to month, but I'm always making progress towards my long-term goals.

Although it can be, a daily routine does not have to be the same set of actions in the same order every single day. It's entirely up to you and your goals.

I'm not trying to convert you into a four a.m. morning person;

I simply want you to be successful in your goal setting. If studying for your MBA every night after the kids are in bed works for you, keep doing it. If working out at lunch is the only way you can make time for your fitness goals, by all means, you do you.

I firmly believe routines are a great way to ensure success, but you have to stick to the plan that you set for yourself, no matter what that plan may look like.

The most crucial part of building a new daily routine is sticking to the plan. At first, it may be difficult because you're going to be battling your old routines, but you need to stick with it.

The more sporadic you are about establishing the new routine, the longer it's going to take for it to become automatic. Remember, we're not just building a daily routine—we're also building new habits, and those require repetition.

Back when I first started Daily New Year's, it was challenging to write every Monday night because I was accustomed to watching TV with my wife after dinner. It was even more difficult to work on the blog in the wee hours of the morning because I was used to sleeping in until seven every day.

After several months of hard work and deliberate routine building, everything became so much easier. As the decisions became almost automatic, the routine took hold. Now I don't even think twice about getting up early. In fact, as I wrap up this chapter, it's 5:08 in the morning.

The past few weeks at work have been extra exhausting, and I'm tired, but I'm also excited to be writing and sharing this content with you. If it had not been for my sticking to my routine and embedding it into my life, I might have never written this book. Sure, some mornings it's difficult to get out

Develop a Daily, Success-Driven Routine

of bed, but my routine keeps me going.

The point is, by building a routine, you reduce decision fatigue, and conserve your willpower and motivation for the long haul.

When you focus on your long-term goals, you need to start with a strong *why* that's going to keep pulling you forward. Then plan and build a daily routine that's going to help get you there, stick to the plan, and watch your momentum grow.

The longer you stick to your routine, the more automatic it will become. Before long, you'll start crushing your goals almost automatically, too.

In the final chapter of this section, we're going to look at the crucial role that momentum plays in our long-term goal-setting success. As you now know, the biggest folly with New Year's resolutions is the starting and stopping and the crashing and burning. In chapter 12, we're going to learn how building momentum crushes that problem.

CHAPTER RECAP

Key Takeaways

- **A routine** is a habitual performance of an established set of actions to the near point of automation.
- Daily routines can help us achieve success with our goals, but they are not meant to automate and roboticize our entire lives. Leave room for adventure and excitement!
- **Routines Reduce Decision Fatigue**
  Having a daily routine can help reduce decision fatigue by allowing us to automate some of our decisions. Waking up early, going to the gym, eating healthy; all of these things can become automatic through routines, leaving decision making power intact for more difficult decisions.
- **Routines Conserve Willpower**
  There's no gauge for measuring willpower, but when we actively push ourselves towards a goal, or we actively resist a temptation, the willpower meter is running. Just like with decision making, routines can help us leave more of our willpower intact for more challenging things.
- **Routines Build Momentum**
  Starting something new isn't very impactful if you keep quitting. Routines allow us to build momentum towards our goals by eliminating the behavior of starting and stopping. Momentum is critical for long-term success in goal setting.
- Because we receive so much new information every day, **our brains store habits** in an effort to reduce overall processing power. **Habits** are how the brain learns to do things without constant

deliberation, and thus routines are created.

✓ If you want to build a robust and success-driven routine that will help to crush your long-term goals, follow these four steps:

1. Identify Your Long-Term Goals
Begin with the end in mind. Identifying your long-term goals can help plan daily actions to support your overall goals.

2. Break Your Goals Down
Break your long-term goals down into daily actions. The more you can break your goals down, the easier it will be to establish a daily routine.

3. Build a Daily Routine Around Your Goals
Once you've broken your goals down into manageable pieces, begin looking for ways to combine your actions into a routine.

4. Stick to the Plan!
The most crucial part of building a new daily routine is sticking to the plan. It will be challenging at first, but the longer you stick to your routine, the more automatic it will become.

Memorable Quotes

☆ *"Starting small, taking action, and building momentum are the keys to success in any endeavor."*

Put it into Practice

↪ Use the corresponding worksheets to build a daily action plan and routine around your long-term goals.

12

Build Momentum Using the Domino Effect

"It does not matter how slowly you go as long as you do not stop."

– Confucius

As we've seen in the previous chapters, becoming a Goal Getter means setting big goals for your life. In some cases, we're talking about big, huge, gigantic goals that are going to take a year, maybe even five years or longer, to complete.

Just the thought of a five-year goal is enough to stop many people, myself included, dead in their tracks. Trying to find a way to achieve a goal that large without planning the steps involved is daunting, and perhaps even impossible.

So far in this section of the book, we've learned how to build a support network for helping to keep ourselves on track and achieving our goals. We've also learned how to use the Four Cs of High Performance to set ourselves up for long-term success and how routines, when used correctly, can help automate some of our goals.

But when we're talking about pursuing our goals for the long haul, how can we be sure to sustain our energy and drive for the road ahead? In the previous chapter I briefly mentioned that routines can help build momentum, allowing your success to grow and compound over time. Now I want to devote an entire chapter to that very topic.

When it comes to goal setting, momentum will be your best and most trusted ally for the long road ahead. Remember, as Goal Getters we don't set one-off resolutions only to quit a few weeks later.

No way!

We take action towards our dreams every single day.

We understand that progress is better than perfection, and that postponing our dreams will only hold us back. We're tired of starting, stopping, and failing. Instead, we need to work towards our goals daily so that we can build massive momentum and become Better Every Day.

Momentum is the key for long-term, sustained success in goal setting; as it builds, it compounds and multiplies your success. We've already looked at momentum through the example of a rocket bound for space, but an even better illustration for momentum can be found in the Domino Effect.

The Domino Effect

As someone who has struggled with resolutions and goal setting in the past, I was fascinated to learn about the power and simplicity of the Domino Effect while reading *The One Thing* by Gery Keller and Jay Papasan.

In their book, Keller and Papasan explain that a domino can

knock over another domino 1.5 times larger than itself. That's 150 percent larger! In a sequence of 13 dominos, the last domino would be 2 billion times larger than the first!

Want to see this in action? Go to YouTube and watch a video entitled "Domino Chain Reaction" by Stephen Morris and prepare to be amazed!

Stephen's video shows the effect in action using some custom-made dominoes, the first of which is only five millimeters tall and one millimeter thick. (Imagine a domino as small as the micro SD card in most smartphones.) Once the first domino is knocked over, it causes a chain reaction and knocks over 10 other dominoes with the last one weighing approximately 110 pounds.

In their book, Keller and Papasan illustrate that, in a chain of dominoes starting with a standard, two-inch domino, the eighteenth domino would be nearly as tall as the Leaning Tower of Pisa. The twenty-third domino be taller than the Eiffel Tower, the thirty-first would surpass Mount Everest, and the fifty-seventh would reach the moon!

With the Domino Effect, things multiply and compound quickly, but why am I explaining this concept to you here, in a book about goal setting?

I only learned about the Domino Effect recently, but back in 2017, I accidentally stumbled onto its powerful simplicity, and since then I've learned to apply the domino effect to goal setting as a whole. Allow me to explain how it all started.

Daily New Year's, My First Domino Experience

As each new year rolls around, I can't help but think about all of the people who set one huge resolution on January first with practically no plan to achieve it. If that sounds like you, it's not your fault; it's what we've been trained to do for generations. And I get it; I used to do the exact same thing.

Setting resolutions may be one of our oldest traditions, but it's a frustrating way to try to achieve success in our lives. For years and years, I like so many others, declared an overly ambitious resolution on January first only to quit by mid-February.

But in 2017, that changed. In October of 2017 I had an epiphany:

> *"Why would I put off self-improvement for most of the year when I could be improving daily? Why do I tend to put off my goals and save them for New Year's Eve when that's failed me time and time again? Why can't I start today, as if today were New Year's Day?"* [1]

These questions lead me to want to improve every day. But even bigger than that, I wanted to inspire as many people as I could to start improving every day, too, but that was a huge goal, and I had no idea how to achieve it.

With my new mission and passion fresh in my mind, I decided that I wanted to build a platform for change—I wanted to start a blog. I was excited about a world of new opportunities, but I had never started a blog before, and I had no idea how much was involved, so I started with a list.

I wrote down every single thing that would have to happen to make that dream a reality. I wrote down my plans for designing the blog, building the website, creating content, promoting it, and on and on.

---

[1] For a deeper look into my story and how Daily New Year's came to be, visit www.dailynewyears.com/about

Build Momentum Using the Domino Effect

I came up with tons of great ideas, but I knew I couldn't do them all at once, so I started prioritizing the steps. I wanted to start a podcast, write a book, create a new goal-setting framework, but I had to start small. I had to find the first domino.

At first, I was worried that I wouldn't be able to maintain a blog for very long, so my first domino was creating a content plan for the first year. To begin with confidence, I needed to know that I could write at least fifty-two blog posts. I came up with five categories that I wanted to cover, alternated them evenly for every Friday in the year, and then filled in a blog topic for each Friday.

It took some time, but once I was finished, I had a concrete plan for a weekly post for the year ahead. It became clear that I could keep my blog going for at least one year, and I was filled with excitement. The Domino Effect had begun.

As I mentioned, I didn't know about the Domino Effect back then. All I knew was that I had a long-term goal of spreading the Daily New Year's message to the world. I started setting small goals that built on each other, that compounded over time, and that built massive momentum in my life.

Fortunately, I managed to stack my goals properly and stay focused for well over a year while I built Daily New Year's, but what if I had tried to start somewhere in the middle? What if I had only given myself one big, ten thousand pound domino? I doubt I could have knocked it over, and I doubt Daily New Year's would exist today.

When I think about New Year's resolutions, I think about one, gigantic domino looming in front of me. Why would I waste my energy trying to knock it over when I could back up, break things down, and tap a tinier domino over and start a chain reaction?

The Domino Effect is a game-changing force for success, and if used properly, we can harness its power to crush our biggest goals.

Crush Your Goals Using the Domino Effect

In my opinion, starting small, taking action, and building momentum are the keys to success in any endeavor. When we quit over and over again, we lose our momentum and that's why the concept of the New Year's resolution doesn't work.

But we don't have to rely on resolutions anymore! We can use the Domino Effect to our advantage. We can plan out our goals and set them up in a way that allows us to build momentum.

Here's what you do:

Write down your biggest goal. What one thing do you want above everything else? What are you excited about? Refer back to **The FOCUSED Framework** if you need to.

Write down every single thing that has to happen to make that goal a reality. If any one item seems too big or too daunting, break it down even further.

Then prioritize the steps and place them in sequential order. What do you need to do first? Second? Third?

Next place all of these smaller, domino goals on your calendar. Maybe your big dream can be achieved in three months, or maybe it's going to take three years. Either way, plan as far in advance as you can.

Finally, once you have your list of domino goals, knock the first one over by doing the first thing on your list.

Build Momentum Using the Domino Effect

- ⊗ Don't wait until New Year's Day.
- ⊗ Don't wait until next month.
- ⊗ Don't even wait until next week.

Knock it over today and get the chain reaction started.

Every time you knock something off the list, you'll see forward progress and your dream will get closer and closer. Excitement will build, and so will your momentum. Soon, you'll be so far along that you won't be able to imagine quitting. Trust me; once you get going and the Domino Effect begins to build in your life, quitting will be the last thing on your mind.

I had the idea for my blog at the gym in October of 2017, and I didn't wait a single day to start. I raced home, bought the domain, and started making a list of everything I needed to do. I created my content calendar and just a short while later in May of 2018, I went live and published my first article. The time between October and May was a blur, but I can tell you that I've been riding the Domino Effect ever since, and my long-term goal of building a world-changing platform is getting closer by the day.

I started small and you can, too. Remember, all you have to do is start. Then it's just a matter of compounding your success every day.

CHAPTER RECAP

Key Takeaways

- When it comes to goal setting, **momentum** will be your best and most trusted ally for the long and exciting road ahead.
- As momentum builds, it compounds and multiplies your success.
- A domino is capable of knocking over other another domino 1.5 times larger than itself. In a chain reaction, this effect adds up to amazing results. This is called **the Domino Effect**, and it's a concept that can be used to crush your goals.
- By breaking our larger goals down into smaller, sequential domino goals, we set ourselves up to build massive momentum in our lives.
- To get started with the Domino Effect, follow these steps:

    1. Write down your biggest goal.
    What one thing do you want above everything else? What are you excited about? Refer back to **The FOCUSED Framework™** if you need to.

    2. Make a list of tasks.
    Write down every single thing that has to happen to make your biggest goal a reality. If any one item seems too big or too daunting, break it down even further.

    3. Prioritize your new domino goals.
    In order to achieve your goal, what do you need to do first? Second? Third? Prioritize the steps and place them in sequential order.

    4. Schedule your domino goals.

Schedule all of your action items in advance and place them on your calendar. Maybe your big dream can be achieved in three months, or maybe it's going to take three years. Either way, plan as far in advance as you can.

5. Knock down your first domino.
Once you have your list of domino goals, knock the first one over by doing the first thing on your list. DO NOT WAIT! Knock that domino over today and get the chain reaction started.

Memorable Quotes

- ☆ *"Starting small and building momentum are the keys to success in any endeavor."*
- ☆ *"Successful goal setting means a daily dedication to the pursuit of your dreams."*

Put it into Practice

- ☞ Use the corresponding worksheets for guided practice in breaking your goals down into domino goals.
- ☞ Go to YouTube and watch Stephen Morris's video, "Domino Chain Reaction."

Rapid Recap: Section 3

Successful goal setting; it's something we're all aiming for.

Goal setting isn't easy, but as I've said before, they're far superior to flash-in-the-pan resolutions that seem to leave us with a bad taste in our mouths. Year after year, we set resolutions, quit, and try again ten months later.

In this chapter, I've strived to give you the tools you're going to need to continue setting goals consistently for years to come. As we've seen, successful goal setting means a daily dedication to the pursuit of your dreams, but it takes focus.

In chapter 9, I taught you how to build a network of support. This network will be a group of people who want to see you succeed in your goal setting. And these relationships will be reciprocal; you're going to want to see your network of people succeed as well.

You can start with a one-on-one accountability partner and

work towards a full Mastermind group or hands-on mentorship. Each group of people can help you in different ways. For people who live in small communities or find themselves to be shy, social communities are also a great place to find accountability and mentorship.

After you've assembled your support team, it's important to remember the Four Cs of High Performance Goal Setting: Competition, Commitment, Completion, and Closure.

In chapter 10, I showed you how goal competition is one of the biggest things keeping you from crushing your goals. When you have too many goals at once, none of them get very far. Once you've narrowed your goals down, you have to commit to them fully. Success can only come from full commitment.

When you're fully committed to your goals, you tend to complete them, but complete means 100 percent; not 99 percent. When we fully complete a goal, we receive a rush of endorphins that tells our brains that achieving our goals feels good. Anything less than 100 percent completion teaches our minds that goal-setting equates hard work and disappointment.

For both the goals you complete and those you don't, you must get closure. Incomplete and abandoned goals create energy anchors that will only drag you down. As you move forward, find closure to keep yourself light for the long goal-setting journey ahead. If you abandon a goal, ask yourself why. The answer is more important than you may realize.

In chapter 11, I made a case for how routines can help you achieve your goals. Routines help us automate some aspects of our goals, leaving more energy in the tank for other things.

Routines help to reduce decision fatigue, conserve our willpower, and build momentum. Routines are a powerful

Rapid Recap

force for progress in your goals, but you don't have to allow routines to kill your spontaneity or sense of adventure. Build routines around your goals and leave the rest of your life open to adventure.

Finally, in chapter 12, I showed you how powerful momentum can be in our lives. Just like interest in the bank, success compounds over time. When we continually start and stop, we kill our momentum, making it more difficult to start over each time.

The Domino Effect allows us to build on our successes. When we break our goals down into smaller pieces, we allow ourselves to start small and build momentum over time. Eventually, we'll have built up so much steam that we won't want to quit.

That's not to say that building momentum will make things failure proof. No, goal setting also has a dark side, too.

Sometimes, things don't go as planned, they take longer than we expected, or we find that a longtime goal is no longer something we want. Sometimes, we have trouble staying motivated, or we fail.

The fourth and final section of this book is dedicated to dealing with difficulties. As they are with everything else, difficulties are inherent to goal setting. Anything in life worth having is worth working hard to have. Nothing good in life comes easy, but that's okay. Our goals and dreams are worth the trouble.

However, I don't want to send you on your way without first arming you with a few strategies for dealing with difficulties along the way. If we're going to be pursuing our goals 365 days a year, we can't allow one small misstep or failure to knock us out of commission—we have to know how to pick ourselves back up and press on.

Crush Your Goals!

In the chapters ahead, I'm going to address the difference between intrinsic and external motivation. What is motivation, really?

I'm also going to give you five powerful tips for overcoming obstacles. With these tips, you'll be dodging problems in no time!

Failure and the fear of failure are the biggest obstacles in goal setting, so I'm also going to teach you how to move beyond failure. Failure often isn't permanent. In fact, it never is. To fail is often the first attempt in learning, and that's just one of the things you're going to learn in chapter 15.

Finally, I'm going to round the book out with a chapter dedicated to taking action towards our dreams. After all, goal setting can't work if we don't start taking action.

With that, let's dive into section four.

Rapid Recap

SECTION 4
DEALING WITH DIFFICULTIES

How to Stay Motivated

"You didn't lose your motivation, you just forgot what you're fighting for."

– Brendon Burchard

Have you ever performed a Google search for "How to stay motivated"?

If you had, you wouldn't be alone. In fact, my research shows that about 3,600 people search that very question every month. [24] It's not just internet searches; I hear people all the time saying, "I just can't seem to get motivated." Let's you and I both admit this together: we've muttered that exact phrase more than once in our lives.

But is finding motivation really the solution?

I would argue that your problem isn't with finding motivation at all. Motivation is easy to get, and it's just as easy to lose. This is yet another glaring problem with New Year's resolutions; the holiday gives us a sudden surge of motivation, but it fades just as quickly as it arrives. Wouldn't you agree?

If you've ever struggled with motivation and searched for a motivational quote or YouTube video, you know the issue I'm talking about here. You get pumped up from the quote or video and jump into your endeavor only to find yourself lacking motivation just a short time later.

One of my favorite quotes about motivation comes from Brendon Burchard. He says, "You didn't lose your motivation; you just forgot what you're fighting for."

Do you see what he's saying there?

Motivation is much more than a simple source of energy; a real motivation is a reason for why you're doing what you're doing.

It's not about how to stay motivated, but rather, what motivates you to begin with. There's a huge difference, so let me unpack this a little bit.

How to Stay Motivated vs. What Motivates Us

I don't want to bore you with dry dictionary definitions, but motivation has two:

"The general desire or willingness of someone to do something" and "The reason or reasons one has for acting or behaving in a particular way." [25]

The former is what I refer to as motivation as an energy source. The latter is what I refer to as motivation as a reason *why*.

In chapter 1, we talked about connecting with your *why*, and that's essentially what we're talking about here. When we have a *why*, or a purpose, our motivation is intrinsic—it comes from deep within us, and it keeps us fully charged for the long-haul.

If you've been finding yourself lacking motivation lately, it could be that you've been using external motivations for energy, and you've likely run the tank dry.

Don't worry; I'll help you connect with your deeper, internal motivations.

Motivation as an Energy Source

External motivation is an excellent tool to get you going, especially when you've just set a brand new goal that you're excited to pursue.

Whether it's losing weight, saving one thousand dollars, or establishing a new personal record in the gym, motivation (aka enthusiasm, drive, ambition, initiative, or determination) will usually get you started with a bang!

The problem is that motivation is fleeting, just like willpower. When you start something new and exciting, motivation comes built in. The feeling is overpowering at first, but when you don't see results quickly enough, you might lose patience, or throw in the towel entirely.

That's when you turn to Google and search for "how to stay motivated." You've exhausted your motivational energy.

There's nothing wrong with using motivation as a means to give you a boost in the beginning, but if we rely on external motivation alone to achieve our goals, we're almost guaranteed to fail.

Why?

There are so many things in life that drain our motivation and willpower. Some days, when things go perfectly well, it can be easy to stay motivated. On other days, you might face some tough situations that drain your energy or sour your mood. When that happens, we have little energy or motivation left to work towards our goals. Some goals take more energy than others, and relying on external motivation alone isn't enough to keep us going on our bad days.

We need something more! We have to look inside ourselves for the answer. Instead of starting with a goal and then looking for motivation, we first need to ask, "What is motivating me to do this?"

If we reconnect with what our motivations were for starting in the first place (also known as our reason *why*), then we can find the energy we need for crushing our most challenging goals!

Motivation as a Reason Why

To further explain the difference between the two types of motivations, allow me to start with an example:

> *Bob loved his job at XYZ Company. He wasn't looking for a new job, but when presented with a job that paid twice as much, he left XYZ Company to pursue a new career at ABC Company. Bob was financially motivated to change jobs. He took the job to earn more money.*

With me so far?

All right, now that we're beginning to separate the two types of motivation, let me ask you this question: What is the reason behind your goal?

Put another way, *why* do you want to achieve your goal?

How to Stay Motivated

What motivated you to set this goal in the first place?

Finding the answer to these questions will help you to find your intrinsic motivation, which is the motivation that stems directly from an action rather than a reward. Intrinsic motivation is doing an activity for its inherent satisfactions rather than for a specific reward or outcome. [26]

Identifying *why* you want to do something is a much more powerful strategy than seeking external motivators.

For example, getting up at four a.m. isn't usually fun for me. Sometimes I work hard over the weekend, and when Monday morning rolls around, I do not want to get out of bed.

When this happens, I have to remind myself that if I were to sleep in, I would miss my morning workout, which affects my overall energy and mood. I also wouldn't get to complete my weekly planning session before heading into the office on Monday morning.

I don't need to seek external motivation to get up and get going in the morning. And that's a good thing, too, because there is no way I'm going to search for a motivational YouTube video at four in the morning.

Instead, I have to recall my motivations for initially setting those goals. I want to work out five days a week, and I want to plan my weekly and daily Big Three goals every Monday morning. To do so, I have to wake up early. It's not an option.

I'll end with another quote to help illustrate my point. This one comes from Dr. Michael Gervais on an episode of the Tim Ferris Show, a podcast I love.

> "We don't need motivation. We need to find ourselves in what's true and honest, and when it matters to us, we'll do whatever it takes." [27]

If your goal truly matters to you, then you should have a reason for pursuing it; you should have a motivation that is driving you forward.

Connect with that reason, write it down where you can see it every day, and you're sure to follow through and achieve success.

"I Can't Seem to Get Motivated."

If you're brand new to goal setting, I hope I've made a solid case for starting with *why* you want to set a goal. Before you embark on a year-long goal, ask yourself, "Why do I want to do this? What is motivating me?"

If the answer isn't a deeply rooted, emotional feeling, then you may face some struggles along the way. **The FOCUSED Framework** can help you work through this early in the goal-setting process, but not all goals will have a strong motivation.

I'm currently training for a half-marathon, and it's not something I feel emotionally connected to. Honestly, I'm not particularly looking forward to it. What motivated me to set this goal? Well, I've cycled a 100-mile race, and I've lifted 1,250 pounds, so I just wanted to add a half marathon to the list.

I just wanted to see if I could do it.

It's not a strong motivation, and most mornings, I don't want to train, but adding this accomplishment to my list is enough to keep me going.

If you're just starting out, make sure to start with motivations that are almost guaranteed to keep you going. If you've been setting goals for a while and you routinely encounter the "I'm just not motivated" problem, you might want to take a step back and look for your intrinsic motivations.

Perhaps you set a goal you're not genuinely passionate about.

I once set a goal to get down to 6 percent body fat. That lasted all of a few months. Though I didn't know it at the time, I didn't honestly want to achieve that goal. Sure, I thought it would be awesome to be shredded, but I like caramel lattes and craft beer too much.

My motivations for that goal were terrible, so I ditched it. Sayonara! However, like I mentioned in chapter 10, I found closure for that goal. I realized that I didn't honestly want to achieve 6 percent body fat and found the closure I needed to move forward free of energy anchors.

If you're struggling with a motivation problem, take a step back and make sure you're pursuing the goals that you're passionate about and that support your dreams. If not, ditch them and begin anew.

However, if you are pursuing the right goals, plaster your reasons *why*, your intrinsic motivations, somewhere you can see them. Sometimes, we forget *why* we started, and we need a reminder. Sometimes, the obstacles we encounter derail our progress and frustrate us to the point of asking, "Why am I even doing this?"

Obstacles are unavoidable. Just like running into road construction during a family vacation, unpleasant things happen. In the next chapter, I'm going to give you five tips for overcoming obstacles. Before we dive into that chapter, be sure to use your workbook's note pages and worksheets to jot down your thoughts and explore your motivations.

I would advise you not to skip these steps. Your motivations are the foundation for which you build your goals. A soft, sandy foundation will certainly spell doom in the future, but goals built on a solid foundation are sure to stand the test of time.

CHAPTER RECAP

Key Takeaways

- **Motivation** is much more than a simple source of energy; a real motivation is a reason for *why* you're doing what you're doing.
- **Motivation has two definitions:**
    1. "The general desire or willingness of someone to do something." (Motivation as an energy source)
    2. "The reason or reasons one has for acting or behaving in a particular way." (Motivation as a reason *why*)
- **Motivation as an Energy Source**
  There's nothing wrong with using motivation as a means to give you a boost in the beginning, but if we rely on external motivation alone to achieve our goals, we're almost guaranteed to fail.
- **Motivation as a Reason *Why***
  Why do you want to achieve your goal? What motivated you to set this goal in the first place? Finding the answer to these questions will help you to find your Intrinsic Motivation.
- **Intrinsic Motivation** is doing an activity for its inherent satisfactions rather than for a specific reward or outcome. Identifying *why* you want to do something is a much more powerful strategy than seeking external motivators.
- If your goal truly matters to you, there should be a driving force—a motivation—that's pulling you forward.
- If you encounter the *"I'm just not motivated"* problem, take a step back and make sure you're pursuing goals that you're passionate about and

that support your dreams. If not, ditch them, find closure, and begin anew with **The FOCUSED Framework™**.

✓ Your motivations are the foundation on which you build your goals. A soft, sandy foundation will certainly spell doom in the future, but goals built on a solid foundation are sure to stand the test of time.

Memorable Quotes

☆ *"You didn't lose your motivation, you just forgot what you're fighting for."* —Brendon Burchard

☆ *"We don't need motivation. We need to find ourselves in what's true and honest, and when it matters to us, we'll do whatever it takes."* —Dr. Michael Gervais

Put it into Practice

↪ Use the accompanying worksheets to identify the reason behind what originally motivated you to set the goals you have. If you're new to goal setting, these worksheets will help you reveal your intrinsic motivations.

↪ If you're struggling to find your Intrinsic Motivation, turn back to Chapter 2: Discover and Embrace Your *Why*. Intrinsic Motivation stems from finding your *why*, so reviewing chapter 2 and its corresponding worksheets may help.

Five Tips for Overcoming Obstacles

"Challenges are gifts that force us to search for a new center of gravity. Don't fight them, just find a new way to stand."

– Oprah Winfrey

How often do you encounter an obstacle or setback in your life? Now before you answer, allow me clarify: I'm not talking about running into a mild traffic jam on the way to work or waking up to find that someone else drank all the milk. While those situations are inconvenient, they aren't major setbacks.

That said, how often do you encounter a setback that seems to derail everything you're trying to do?

Maybe you're trying to save up enough money to buy a car but you lose your job? Or perhaps you're trying to start your career but can't seem to land your first official job after college? Maybe you finally landed your dream job only to find that your personal relationships are suffering or that the job isn't at all what you expected?

Crush Your Goals!

I don't mean to be all "doom and gloom" here, but in life, things happen and they're not always the fun, positive, upbeat things we imagine for ourselves.

Back in chapter four I told a short story about a job I lost at an early age. I want to tell a slightly longer version of that story here because at the time it was one of the scariest setbacks I had experienced in my life. My wife and I were newly married at nineteen, we were both paying our own way through college, and we had just bought our first house. We were living the dream and making it all on our own. It was fantastic!

It was fantastic until I lost my job, that is. I was working in construction as a laborer for a brick laying company. Things were going well, the job was almost done, and I was looking forward to the next job site. What were we going to build next?

I hadn't stopped to consider that maybe the owner of the company didn't have a *next* job lined up. I hadn't stopped to consider that I was the youngest guy on the crew and the last one to be hired. I didn't understand that, in construction, when there weren't any jobs on the books, people were laid off. It was typical of the industry, but I didn't know that, and I certainly didn't appreciate it at the time. My wife and I had just achieved one of our goals by buying a house, and now we were facing the difficult reality of not being able to pay our bills.

As I mentioned back in chapter four, I was perturbed to say the least. Overall, I had a terrible attitude about the situation. I resented the owner of that company, and I felt betrayed. Over and over again I wondered, "How could he do this to me?"

At nineteen years old I was proud of myself. I felt grown up and mature. I was in college, newly married, gainfully employees, and I was a homeowner. Everything seemed to

Five Tips for Overcoming Obstacles

being going great until I hit this (what felt like a major) setback. I was scared, stressed, worried, and felt nearly hopeless. This was a brand new problem for my wife and me.

I never stopped to think about what my boss must have felt like. Sure, I was responsible for making my mortgage payment, but he was responsible for running an entire company and keeping as many employees working as he could. For him, not having a new job lined up was one hundred times the setback I was experiencing. But at nineteen, I couldn't see past my own situation because it felt too big to manage.

Fortunately, in spite of my bad attitude, my wife helped me to see a way for overcoming this setback. She was working as a server at Applebees at the time and assured me that I could do the same thing. I didn't want to be a server. I didn't have people skills. I wasn't outgoing. (Note the negative self-talk I've since overcome.) I just wanted a job behind the scenes. But I was desperate. I had been without a job for several weeks and the bills weren't going to pay themselves, so I applied at Olive Garden. It took a couple of weeks to get a callback and an interview, but I eventually took a job as a server.

Obstacle overcame. Crisis avoided.

As it turns out, I ended up being pretty good at being a server, and I learned a ton of life skills along the way. I learned how to budget and save money from a cash-based job. I learned how to interact with customers, how to work as a team, how to juggle my priorities as my schedule changed week to week, and so, so much more. That job was great for me, and I wouldn't change anything from my two years there.

Since then I've encountered setback after setback and obstacle after obstacle. Some were easy to overcome, some were not. Some felt small, and some felt like the end of the world. Some felt like massive setbacks at the time, but then years later, were blips on the radar, nearly forgotten with the passing of time.

Regardless of the individual setbacks I've experienced throughout the years, I've learned that avoiding every setback that might come along is impossible. Sometimes they are momentary roadblocks that have the potential to ruin a weekend, and sometimes they are significant obstacles that may prevent us from achieving our biggest goals.

Perhaps obstacles seem to be a consistent part of your life, always popping up and getting in the way. Or maybe things typically go pretty well for you, but you've suddenly had your first run-in with a significant setback or failure. Either way, setbacks are a very real part of life, and overcoming them is a necessary skill for successful goal setting.

Trust me; you cannot set life-changing goals and not run into a problem or two every once in a while. The sooner you can acknowledge that setbacks are going to happen, the sooner you can put a plan in place for overcoming them.

If you do some Googling, you will find that there are several methods that you can use to get yourself back on track after experiencing a setback, but the following five strategies have always worked best for me, and I want to share them with you.

1. Plan for the Worst. Hope for the Best.

Setbacks are inevitable; there's no way around it. No matter how skilled or talented you are, something will go wrong in your life at some point, especially if you're trying something new or challenging.

Successful people don't become successful by avoiding obstacles; they become successful by learning to expect obstacles and then face them head on.

Everything is easier to deal with if you're expecting it. That's why I always say, "Plan for the worst but hope for the best."

This thought process isn't meant to be pessimistic, and I'm not suggesting that you walk around with a negative world view. Planning for the worst is intended to help you mentally prepare for the possibility that something may go wrong.

When you prepare for the worst, you remove the power that a bad situation has over you because you're better equipped to see it coming. If you're unprepared for a setback, then it's much more likely to derail and discourage you, which may cause you to give up in a moment of weakness.

Being prepared, however, allows you to more easily see that there's almost always another way to achieve your goal, given enough time, effort, and determination. Had I acknowledged losing my job was a possibility back when I was nineteen, I wouldn't have been so blindsided by the situation. Since then, however, I've learned that lesson and I use it to plan for the worst. Years later I lost another job due to a layoff, but that time I was mentally prepared for it. I knew that I could land on my feet once again and I did.

I love my current job, but occasionally I can't help but think, "What would I do if I lost my job today?" While that may seem like a gloomy attitude to have, it helps remind me that setbacks happen from time to time. Better yet, it helps me plan for the worst, but I'm always hoping for the best. As you plan your goals, try your best to do the same and when you encounter a setback, it won't have nearly as much power over you.

2. Limit Your Disappointment

Not hitting your goal quickly enough, or not achieving it at all, can be extremely disappointing, and the longer you've spent striving for a goal, the more upsetting it is when you miss the mark.

Worst of all, disappointment is a toxic feeling. The longer you ruminate and dwell on disappointment, the more it will disrupt your ability to focus on your other goals. It's important to acknowledge your feelings and your frustration, but most experts say that we should limit the amount of time we allow ourselves to feel disappointed.

When I lost my job I was disoriented, and I was at a total loss. I knew I needed to look for a new job as soon as possible, but I was too distracted by my misfortune that I didn't know where to start. I was angry and scared, so I couldn't help but ruminate on the problem. Fortunately my wife had a great idea that saw us through the situation.

When we dwell on our misfortunes, we waste massive amounts of energy that we could be using to achieve our goals, and when this happens, we're more likely to give up altogether. But it's not always easy to snap out of it, especially if you're on your own. Over the years I've learned to spot this behavior early on, and I can begin to pull myself out of the trap, but if you're just beginning to try this strategy for overcoming disappointment you may need a few ideas to get you started.

The next time you feel disappointed, work on reducing the amount of time you dwell on the situation using some or all of the following tips:

- ⊘ Call a friend or mentor and talk it through with them. Get some outside perspective on your situation. Often times, talking about the problem out loud will help you accept it and move on more quickly.

Five Tips for Overcoming Obstacles

- ✓ Time block your dwelling by allowing yourself to dwell for no more than one hour.
- ✓ Give yourself a pep talk. Tell yourself that you need to move on, that you're human, and you're allowed to make mistakes or experience setbacks.
- ✓ If all else fails, find a way to distract yourself until you can calm down and reexamine things with a clear mind.

The faster you can focus on the positives and move past the problem, the quicker you can get back to achieving success in your life. I've seen people allow disappointment to keep them down for weeks (been there, done that), and sometimes even months. All this does is keep you from moving forward with your other goals and ambitions.

It's easier said than done, and it takes practice, but work towards becoming faster at bouncing back from disappointing failures—it's a skill that will serve you for years to come.

3. Learn From Your Mishaps

John Maxwell often says, "Sometimes you win. Sometimes you learn," which is an adaptation from the old saying, "Sometimes you win. Sometimes you lose." [1]

Like I mentioned earlier in the book, obstacles and setbacks are not failures; they are simply a problem that we need to overcome. One great way to overcome problems is to look for a lesson in the perceived failure and then apply that to your next attempt.

What can you learn from the experience? What could you have done better, or what should you have not done? What can you improve upon so that you have a better chance for

---

[1] John Maxwell has a book entitled Sometimes You Win--Sometimes You Learn: Life's Greatest Lessons Are Gained from Our Losses.

success the next time around?

After my untimely termination, I learned how to better manage my emotions, and that I was responsible for how I react to negative situations. I learned that I'm not the only one with problems, and that I'm strong enough to bounce back. I learned that sometimes the job you don't want is the one that teaches you the most. I learned a ton from that season in my life, but the biggest lesson I learned is that you have to learn from your mishaps and misfortunes.

You've heard this before, but I'll remind you again: If at first you don't succeed, try again. However, before you do, be sure to take a hard look at your situation and try to learn something new. Obstacles and failures are the steps by which you build your success. When you run into a setback or an obstacle, use the opportunity to build a new step. Keep climbing and success will be yours. (More on this in the next chapter.)

4. Focus on Being Better Every Day

Goals aren't about being perfect; they're about being better than you were before. Remember that quote from Elyse Lyons, The Savvy Sagittarius?

When we're looking at overcoming obstacles, setbacks, or even disappointment, we have to remember that even if we don't achieve our goal, or if it's taking way longer than expected, or if life has sent us down a new, unexpected path, the act of trying alone is making us better than we were before.

If you're trying to save money, but emergencies keep popping up to deplete your savings, think about where you would be if you didn't have your savings to fall back on. You would probably be getting deeper into credit card debt with every new emergency. An empty savings account is much better than going deeper in debt, right?

Five Tips for Overcoming Obstacles

If you're fifteen pounds short of your weight loss goal but you're eating better and working out consistently, aren't you already healthier than you were before? Being healthier than you were is better than achieving your exact goal weight, wouldn't you agree?

If you find yourself feeling letdown, be sure to look on the bright side. Like Elyse said, goals aren't about being perfect; they're about being better than you were before.

5. Understand that You Only Fail if You Quit

If you're currently facing a massive obstacle in your life, overcoming it may seem impossible. For many people, hitting a wall feels a lot like failure, so they immediately quit or turn in another direction.

But if we're going to be high-achieving Goal Getters, one critical thing we have to understand is that obstacles only become failures when we accept them as failures.

In my story, I didn't have much of a choice; I had to get a new job to keep paying my bills. The solution to your situation may not be as clear, especially at first, but give it time.

When faced with an obstacle, don't view it as a failure. Instead, look for another way around the problem. Remember the old adage, "Where there's a will; there's a way"? It's never been truer than it is with goal setting.

When you truly want something, there's always another way to achieve it, even in spite of things standing in your way. All you have to do is keep trying. You only fail when you quit trying.

Become an Overcomer

Overcoming obstacles is vital to successful goal setting.

In fact, how you deal with disappointment could be an accurate predictor of your ability to be successful in life. If you quit every time you face a roadblock or a setback, your ability to be successful is going to be significantly reduced. It's harsh, but true.

It's common for kids to want to quit something in school. Whether it's a sport like football or basketball, or it's a fine art like band or drama, kids often come to a point where they want to quit. Maybe practice is too much work, or perhaps the activity is too competitive. Maybe it's not as easy as they thought it would be.

Either way, there's an old saying that parents used to tell their kids at this critical point: "If you quit now, you're going to be a quitter the rest of your life." Maybe this draconian advice is less common today, but I certainly remember my dad telling me this when I wanted to quit the baseball team in high school.

The fact is, there will be things you need to quit. As you try new things in life, you're going to come across some things you don't enjoy. If that's the case, don't stick it out just to stick it out.

On the other hand, if giving up is your default reaction any time something gets difficult, you may never see your goals or dreams realized. Quitting gets easier and easier as time goes on. Be aware of this trap and avoid it at all costs.

Overcoming obstacles isn't easy, but like anything else, the only way to improve is through practice, practice, practice. Each time you overcome a challenge, you build confidence and mental toughness for the challenges that still lie ahead. You prove to yourself that you can thrive in spite of life's curveballs, that you're not a quitter—you're an overcomer.

However, every once in a while, a setback may feel too big.

Five Tips for Overcoming Obstacles

Sometimes, setbacks can feel like total failure. In the next chapter, we're going to explore what you can do if you think you've failed. I'm going to attempt to change how you perceive failure as well as how to move beyond failure. With any luck, I might even succeed in changing your definition of failure altogether.

CHAPTER RECAP

Key Takeaways

- ⊘ Setbacks are a very real part of life, and overcoming them is a necessary skill for successful goal setting.
- ⊘ The sooner you can acknowledge that setbacks are going to happen, the sooner you can put a plan in place for overcoming them. These five strategies can help:

  1. **Plan for the Worst. Hope for the Best.**
     Successful people don't become successful by avoiding obstacles; they become successful by learning to expect obstacles and then they face them head-on.
  2. **Limit Your Disappointment.**
     When we dwell on our misfortunes, we waste enormous amounts of energy that we could be using to achieve our goals. The faster you can focus on the positives and move past the problem, the quicker you can get back to achieving success in your life.
  3. **Learn From Your Mishaps.**
     One great way to overcome problems is to look for a lesson in the perceived failure and then apply it to your next attempt. What can you learn from the experience?
  4. **Focus on Being Better Every Day.**
     We have to remember that even if we don't achieve our goal, or if it's taking way longer than expected, the act of trying alone is making us better than we were before.
  5. **Understand that You Only Fail if You Quit.**
     Obstacles are only failures when we accept them as failures and then give up. When faced

Five Tips for Overcoming Obstacles

- with an obstacle, don't view it as a failure. Look for another way around the problem.
- **How you deal with disappointment** could be an accurate predictor of your ability to be successful in life. If you quit every time you encounter a setback, your ability to be successful is going to be significantly reduced.
- Sometimes there are things we have to quit. If that's the case, don't stick it out just to stick it out. Be sure to **validate your reasons for quitting**, because quitting only gets easier and easier if done for the wrong reasons.

Memorable Quotes

☆ *"Sometimes you win. Sometimes you learn."* —John C. Maxwell

☆ *"Goals aren't about being perfect; they're about being better than you were."* —Elyse Lyons

Put it into Practice

- [ ] The next time you feel disappointed, work on reducing the amount of time you dwell on the situation.
- [ ] The next time you experience a failure, look for a lesson learned and apply that knowledge to your next attempt.
- [ ] Looking at your goals, what are some obstacles you might encounter? How might you overcome them should they arise? Plan ahead and get prepared.
- ➦ Use the corresponding worksheets for guided practice on overcoming your obstacles.

Moving Beyond Failure

"Failure is so important. We speak about success all the time. It is the ability to resist failure or use failure that often leads to greater success."

– J.K. Rowling

As we near the end of this book, I want to round out one of the most important, recurring topics found in these pages: failure.

Back in chapter 2, I outlined the six most common fears of goal setting, with the fear of failure being one of the most prevalent. It's no secret that most people don't want to fail. Trust me; I don't want to fail any more than you do. I'm sure that the most successful people in the world were, at one point, afraid to fail, and I'm even more confident that they did fail from time to time.

In the previous chapter, I made the point that you can't fail as long as you don't quit. I don't want to sound hypocritical in this chapter, but I'm also not naive. I firmly believe that, as long as you keep trying to achieve your goals, you cannot fail. Maybe you won't achieve your exact goal, but as long as you're trying, you're becoming Better Every Day.

However, sometimes, things happen that are well beyond our control. Perhaps a recession kills your business. That would certainly feel like a failure. Maybe you've spent two years working on a blog or a book that no one is reading. That might feel like a failure, too.

So yes, I admit that failure is an unavoidable part of life, but it doesn't have to paralyze us or stop us from shooting for our dreams. Everyone fears failure at one point or another, so I want to show you how to move forward in spite of that fear. I also want to help you redefine failure by looking at it as an opportunity to learn instead of a negative outcome or reason to quit.

Moving Forward in Spite of the Fear of Failure

When I began writing this book, I knew there was a chance that I may not sell a single copy beyond the copies purchased by my wonderful family and friends.

Spoiler alert: I wrote this book anyway because it was one of my dreams. That's what this chapter is all about: forgetting about failure and moving forward in spite of fear.

As we saw back in chapter 10, Only 20 percent of people bother to set goals for themselves on a regular basis. That means that only one in five people even bother to try. Perhaps the act of not trying is a fantastic strategy for avoiding failure? You can't fail if you don't try, right?

Wrong! Here's the truth: If you're not trying to reach new levels in your life, you're already failing. You're failing to grow. You're failing to reach your full potential. You're failing to live life to its fullest.

You didn't buy this book so that you could read these pages and then go back to not trying. If you've made it this far into the book, I can tell that you're someone who has big goals and even bigger dreams for your life. You cannot allow the fear of failure hold you back from those dreams. Yes, you can be afraid; that's completely normal. However, you cannot allow that fear to stop you from trying.

If you follow the strategies and advice found within this book, trying new things, setting goals, and taking action will soon be hard-wired into your Goal Getter's DNA. As someone seeking to become Better Every Day, it's critical that you forget about failure and instead, focus on your goals.

Henry Ford once said, "Obstacles are those frightful things you see when you take your eyes off your goal."

I love this quote because it points to the fact that if we look for everything that might go wrong, we're sure to see plenty of things that might go wrong. Instead, we need to forget about failure and focus all of our attention on the countless ways we can crush our goals.

Why Worry?

As a young kid and early teen, I was a tremendous worrier; I stressed about everything. But as I've gotten older, I've tried to live by the idea that if something is beyond my control, I can't allow myself to worry about it. However, if the outcome is something I can influence or control, then I should do everything within my power to reach my desired outcome.

In other words, if you can do something about it, do it. If you can't, then why worry about it?

You can't control the weather, right? Then why worry about it? You can, however, plan around the weather. If it looks like rain, bring an umbrella, or if it's going to be freezing cold, dress in comfortable layers.

I see people all of the time worrying about countless things that are well beyond their control; the weather, traffic, the stock market, or what might happen tomorrow. Many times, they spend so much time worrying about things they can't control that they forget to work towards the things they can control.

The point is, as we set goals and take action towards our dreams, some degree of failure is certainly possible, but you shouldn't worry about it. If you can do something to prevent it, do it. If you can't, then worrying about potential failure isn't going to help you; it's only going to weigh you down.

If you can't stop worrying about potential failure, then let's completely redefine what it means to fail.

First Attempt in Learning: Failure as an Opportunity

As I illustrated in the previous chapter, you cannot fail as long as you're trying because if you're trying, you're learning. If you're taking chances and setting goals, you're already doing more than most people.

Remember, four out of five people are not setting goals. When you go to work or school tomorrow, look around. Most of those people will never have the opportunity to fail because they're never going to risk trying something new. You're ahead of the game, my friend!

Yes, failure is almost inevitable at some point or another, but failure doesn't have to be a dream killer. Instead, it can be a fantastic learning opportunity.

There is an acronym for FAIL that stands for First Attempt In

Moving Beyond Failure

Learning. Unless we decide to quit and bury our heads in the sand, failing is simply the beginning of the learning process, and that's the opportunity that the four out of five people who aren't setting goals are missing.

To use a classic example, if you touch a hot stove and burn your hand, you know not to touch a hot stove again. The same is true in life and of our mishaps. If we take a step back and learn from failure, then we can come up with a better, stronger plan for moving forward.

Thomas Edison once said, "I haven't failed. I've just found ten thousand ways that don't work." He said this because of how many times he failed in perfecting the incandescent light bulb. Edison may not have been the original inventor of electric light, but after testing more that six thousand possible materials, he landed on carbonized bamboo, making his light bulb the first commercially practical incandescent light. [28]

Instead of quitting, he recorded the first failure as one way an efficient, household lightbulb would not work. Then he tried a second method and a third. The more attempts he made, the more ways he discovered not to create a long-lasting light bulb. As he continued to try and fail, he continued to learn, and on October 22, 1879, he and his team succeeded in creating a bulb that would last 13.5 hours. [29] Edison's success meant ruling out countless ways that didn't achieve his goal of creating an inexpensive household lightbulb that would last a long time.

Edison and his team went on to create hundreds of other inventions that largely impacted our world today. His creations included the movie camera, microphone, and phonograph. Sure, overcoming failure is a critical skill for becoming a successful inventor, but can you imagine where we would be as a society if Edison had quit as a response to his first failure? Instead, Edison and his team embodied the spirit of using failure as a first attempt in learning.

When things are going well, it's tough to audit what we're doing right. We can chalk our success up to luck, or we can assume that we're doing everything right. But when we fail, we're offered the opportunity to examine what didn't work and make improvements to our strategy.

The mistake that many people make is quitting when they hit a roadblock, but doing so creates a missed opportunity to learn something valuable. If you want to be successful with long-term goal setting, it's important to get comfortable with learning from failure. That may seem counterintuitive, but you have a much better chance of becoming successful if you can learn how to triumph over failure and begin failing forward.

Failing Forward

In chapter 1, I talked about finding your *why*. When your *why* is big enough, any amount of failure shouldn't be enough to stop you from crushing your goal. As a kid, most of us learn to ride bikes. It's fun, everyone is doing it, and it would be a huge bummer to be the only kid on the block who couldn't ride a bike. That's why we all get back on the bike even after we crash and scrape our knees.

Crashing hurts, but with every fall, we learn something new about riding a bike. We learn how to balance our body weight, when to make steering adjustments with the handlebars, and how to adjust our speed for turning. This process is what it means to fail forward.

If we gave up after our first crash, we would never learn those crucial lessons. We can say the same thing for walking, running, swimming, or any number of things. So why would we not apply the failing forward principle to other aspects of our lives?

As you move forward with goal setting, there will be instances that feel like total failures. If you take these opportunities to learn something new and use them to move forward more intelligently, then I would say that if you're failing at all, at least you're failing forward.

The Success Staircase

When we look at successful people, it's easy to imagine that they had an easy path or a shortcut to the top. I can assure you that this is never the case. There is never a straight path or an elevator to success. Instead, you have to build a staircase to reach the success you desire.

As you overcome setbacks, avoid obstacles, and conquer failures, you begin to build steps upon everything you've learned. Imagine encountering a setback and finding a way to overcome it. When you do this, you learn a valuable new lesson, and that lesson becomes a solid new step for which you can use to reach a new level.

And because you're building your staircase from lessons you've learned, only you can see your staircase. As you move past more and more obstacles, your staircase grows taller and taller, allowing you to reach higher levels of success. One day, you'll have climbed so high that others will begin to look up at you, and wonder how you achieved such heights so quickly.

They won't be able to see the staircase that you built on countless failures and lessons learned. They'll assume your success came free and easy, but you'll know the truth. You'll know that you've worked hard to get where you are. You'll know that you fought your way forward through fear and failure, and no one can take that away from you.

So What Will You Do?

You've come a long way since the beginning of this book. You've learned how to get started with goal setting, how to cultivate a Goal Getter's mindset, and how to build a strong system for long-term success.

In the end, you've also learned how to deal with the difficulties that lie ahead. Will you allow the fear of failure to hold you back, or will you use what you've learned and take action towards your dreams?

If you've made it this far into this book, there's no doubt about it; you're a Goal Getter through and through, and I have full faith and confidence that you're going to do amazing things in your life.

You have what it takes to set goals and become Better Every Day. You have dreams for your life, and now you have all the tools you need to start seeing those dreams come true.

There's only one thing left to do: Take action.

Moving Beyond Failure

CHAPTER RECAP

Key Takeaways

- As a general rule, you cannot fail as long as you continue to try. However, because nothing is a guarantee, we're going to fail from time to time.

  These concepts and ideas will help you move forward in spite of the fear of failure:

- **You cannot avoid failure by refusing to try new things.** If you're not trying to reach new levels in your life, you're already failing. You're failing to grow. You're failing to reach your full potential. You're failing to live life to its fullest.

- If we look for everything that might go wrong, we're sure to see plenty of things that might go wrong. Instead, we need to **forget about failure** and **focus all of our attention** on the countless ways we can crush our goals.

- **Why worry about potential failure?** If you can do something to influence the outcome, by all means, do it. If you can't, then worrying about the outcome will only drain your energy and weigh you down.

- **FAIL stands for First Attempt In Learning.** When we fail, we're offered the opportunity to examine what didn't work and make improvements to our strategy. When we quit prematurely, we miss a valuable lesson to learn.

- **Learn how to Fail Forward.** If you do fail, be sure to keep your momentum and keep moving forward. We all learn how to walk by repeatedly falling.

- **There is never a straight path or an elevator to success.** You have to build your own staircase. As you overcome setbacks, avoid obstacles, and conquer failures, you begin to build steps out of everything you've learned, and those steps help you to reach new levels in your life.

Memorable Quotes

- ☆ *"Obstacles are those frightful things you see when you take your eyes off your goal." —*Henry Ford
- ☆ *"I haven't failed. I've just found 10,000 ways that don't work." —*Thomas Edison

Put it into Practice

- ☐ Think back to some of the things you've regarded as failures in your life. Were they truly failures? What did you learn? How can you use those failures to improve going forward?
- ☐ Take some time to reflect and try to apply the concepts from this chapter to your life, both retroactively and in moving forward onto bigger and better things.
- ➮ Use the corresponding worksheets for guided practice and reflection.
- ➮ Be sure to use the notes pages to capture the thoughts from your reflection.

Take Action Today!

"The path to success is to take massive, determined actions."

—

Tony Robbins

You have big dreams for your life, right? Don't you want to see those dreams come true?

Of course, you do! You're nearly finished reading this book—a book about ditching resolutions and crushing goals all year long.

I'm so thankful that you've read my book. I've worked hard on it so that you and other people like you can learn to identify, set, and crush goals that will ultimately lead to the life you've been dreaming of.

I hope you'll agree that there's a ton of great information within these pages, but here's the deal: all of the learning in the world will not help you achieve success if you don't take action on what you've learned.

There are countless books, podcasts, articles, videos, seminars, and online courses dedicated to helping people find success. In fact, all of those resources combined make the personal development industry worth approximately ten billion dollars.

With numbers like that, it's safe to say that just about everyone wants to be more successful, but if personal development were the key to success, wouldn't the people spending the ten billion dollars be well on their way to achieving sweet, sweet success? I mean, they're learning a lot, so they have to be, right?

I wish!

A few years ago, a close friend and mentor of mine introduced me to my first personal development book, *The Compound Effect* by Darren Hardy, and since then, I've been a relatively large contributor to that ten billion dollar industry. That booked got me hooked on personal development! (Thanks, DC!)

Maybe you're the same way. Perhaps you love reading book after book, watching hours of educational videos, and tuning into the latest episodes of your favorite podcasts. That's fantastic! Not many people are doing what you're doing.

I'm a huge fan of investing in personal development, but again, all of the learning in the world wouldn't help us achieve success if we never take action towards our dreams. Another book on the shelf won't change our lives.

I used to read book after book about goal setting, success, leadership, and so on. I took pride in reading these types of books, and I believed that learning from them was making me more successful almost automatically. Boy, was I wrong!

After every book I read, I would feel a strong sense of

accomplishment. I would close the book, return it to the shelf, and finally, I would jot down the date that I finished it on my annual reading list. Then, without much thought, I would start reading the next book on my list. I never took action on the content I was reading, and I rarely applied the information to my life. I certainly never took the time to put in the work or complete the action prompts.

You see, I had a goal for reading a certain number of books each year, and I was only reading to satisfy that goal. A few years ago, though, that all changed. When I realized that I was reading for book count and not for actual development and growth, I changed course. I realized that success could only be obtained when we combine what we learn with taking massive action on what we've learned.

So I decided to start putting in the work; I decided to start taking action.

That's why this book is so different than most. It was written and designed to be the first and last book you will ever need to start identifying, setting, and crushing your goals.

Every chapter included a recap, a corresponding notes section for your thoughts, and guided worksheets that hopefully helped you process and utilize the information found in each chapter. If you completed them, kudos!

If you skipped over those pages in your workbook (like I would have done not so long ago), please go back and revisit them. Dive into them with extreme focus and use them to your advantage.

This book wasn't written just to teach you about setting goals—it was written to help you take your life from where you are right now to where you want to go. With that in mind, I implore you to start taking action towards your dreams today. If you haven't already, start setting goals as soon as you reach the end of this book. Don't wait!

Hopefully, you're feeling fired up right now, and you're ready to take action. Hopefully you're ready to start setting some massive goals in your life. I don't know where you want your life to go; I just know that goal setting is the perfect, all-terrain vehicle to take you there.

As I write the final pages of this book, I can't help but get excited about the possibilities you now face in your life. The moment I decided to stop postponing my life, the moment I decided to ditch my resolutions and instead started setting daily goals for myself, was the day my life changed forever.

I'm excited that this could be that day in your life!

This could be the day that your dreams start coming true, but it's up to you. You could return this book to the shelf and tell yourself that you're going to start next week or next month. You could even wait for New Year's Eve to roll around again.

Or you could take action today.

You could close this book and open a new, blank journal where you could start describing your dream life. You could write out your long-term goals, and you could begin to break them down into yearly, quarterly, monthly, weekly, and daily goals. You could start taking action towards your dreams right here and right now.

Either way, it's up to you, but you better decide fast because you're running out of pages. This book is nearly finished, and your mind is probably racing.

Maybe you feel like there is so much more to learn. Trust me; you don't need to learn anything else. You know everything you need to know to get started right now. The feeling that you need to learn more is just your mind's way of helping you procrastinate.

Take Action Today!

Maybe you're still struggling with fear or self-limiting beliefs. Please hear me when I say, YOU'VE GOT THIS! Whatever goals you're about to set, you're going to crush. You're a Goal Getter now!

You don't rely on New Year's resolutions to get started—you don't wait for next month, next week, or even tomorrow. You take action towards your dreams every single day, starting today.

You understand that progress is better than perfection, and that postponing your dreams will only hold you back. You're tired of starting, stopping, and failing—you're better than that.

From now on, you're going to work towards your goals with a passionate, unstoppable momentum.

You and I, we're Goal Getters, and we're only one goal away from achieving GREATNESS in our lives!

So what do you say?

Are you ready to set some goals and see your dreams come true?

You've got this!

Now, go Crush Your Goals!

CHAPTER RECAP

Key Takeaways

- The personal development industry is worth approximately ten billion dollars, but investing in personal development content does not guarantee your success unless you put in the work. **You cannot buy success.**
- All of the learning in the world won't help us achieve success if we never **take action** towards our dreams.
- Success can only be obtained when we combine what we learn with **taking massive action** on what we've learned.
- Watch out for self-limiting beliefs that tell you that you don't know enough to get started.
- You know everything you need to know to get started right now. The feeling that you need to learn more is just your mind's way of helping you procrastinate.

Put it into Practice

Every chapter included a recap, a notes section for your thoughts, and guided worksheets that hopefully helped you process and utilize the information found in each chapter.

- If you skipped over those pages, please go back and revisit them. **Dive into them with extreme focus** and use them to your advantage.
- ☐ Tell yourself that you know enough to get started today, and that you're more than good enough Crush Your Goals!
- ☐ Decide to stop postponing your goals and dreams and decide to take action today.

Take Action Today!

- [ ] Recite the Goal Getter's Creed:

    I am a Goal Getter.

    I don't rely on New Year's Resolutions to get started—I don't wait for next month, next week, or even tomorrow. I take action towards my dreams every single day.

    I understand that progress is better than perfection, and that postponing my dreams will only hold me back. I'm tired of starting, stopping, and failing—I'm better than that.

    I'm going to work towards my goals with a passionate, unstoppable momentum.

    I am a Goal Getter, and I'm only one goal away from achieving GREATNESS in my life!

- Use the corresponding worksheets to help build a bulletproof action plan using the core principles from the previous chapters. Then, take massive action!

Epilogue

Writing this book has taken me on an incredible journey. What I once thought would be a long-term, five-year goal is now complete.

When I started the year in 2019, I had no idea that writing a book would be so much work but at the same time so achievable.

What I once thought would be nearly impossible was something I managed to do in less than a year. It makes me wonder, what else seems impossible now but might prove doable with enough focus and determination? Maybe you're thinking the same thing, too?

I once thought that writing a book would be one of the hardest things I would ever do, and maybe along the way it felt like my hardest thing. I've read dozens of books and thought, "How did they write three hundred pages about this topic?"

Now I realize that with passion comes purpose, and with a purpose comes a person's life work. I hope you can tell from reading this book that goal setting is one of my biggest passions, and I hope this book is the beginning of my life's work.

I love goal setting and I love achievement for achievement's sake. I love being able to say that I've lifted 1,250 pounds, that I've cycled 100 miles, and that I've ran 13.1 miles. For many, those are small things. For others, those may seem impossible. The beauty of goal setting is that it's all about your own personal journey. No two people's lives are the same.

As you start setting lifelong goals for yourself, and as you start building towards your dream life, please remember that it's your journey and no one else's. You have to run your own race. You have to be your own person.

Lastly, remember that goal setting isn't about perfection; it's about being better than you were before. You're going to run into problems and setbacks along the way, but don't give up. I struggled with this book for over a year. I was splitting time between too many goals and I was frustrated.

Then I discovered my problem: goal competition, one of the Four Cs from chapter 10. I decided to put my blog and podcast on hold for several months to pursue this book. That was tough, super tough, but I had closure on the blog and podcast goals. I knew that as soon as the book was complete, I'd return to those passion projects. That helped me eliminate a couple of energy anchors and competing goals.

Now that this book is complete, I can return to Daily New Year's knowing I've achieved one of my life's biggest goals. I wish the same for you.

As you pursue goal setting, you're going to learn along the way. You're going to encounter things you wish you had

Epilogue

known years ago. Be patient with the process and with yourself. At the beginning of this year, I didn't know about the Four Cs but now they're helping to guide my goals and I'm writing about them in my book. That's exciting!

So again, be patient with yourself. That's one of the biggest keys to long-term success. I need to remind myself of that as much as I want you to hear it, too.

Now that my book is complete, I have other goals to return to. I'm getting back to the blog, I want to start a YouTube channel, and I need to start working towards that five-year public speaking goal. Depending on when you're reading this, who knows what I will have achieved, but one thing is for sure: I'll be forever grateful that our paths crossed here in these pages.

I'm concluding this book with high hopes that it changes lives. If my message has changed your life, I would be honored if you'd share your story with me. Please visit www.crushyourgoalsbook.com and drop me a line. Trust me; your story will make my day and I can't wait to hear it.

Here's to hoping our paths cross again soon,

Cheers!

Austin

Acknowledgments

This book was one of my life's biggest achievements to date, and it was a goal that took hundreds of hours, countless four a.m. mornings, and dozens of gallons of coffee to see it to fruition.

As with many goals, very few things of great significance can be achieved on our own. To write this book, I needed more than coffee to achieve my goal; I needed any army of family and friends behind me, supporting me, and cheering me on.

I want to thank all of the people who helped me see this dream goal come true.

To my loving wife and best friend, Callie. A person could ask for no better partner to experience all that life has to offer. Your compassion for people, your huge, caring heart, and your kind, loving spirit are the things I love most about you. You inspire me.

When I get lost in the future, in the things that could be, you keep me grounded, not as an anchor, but as a reminder that being mindful and present are just as important as striving for the future. You're the why for every goal I set. You're my motivation.

Crush Your Goals!

You've always been my biggest supporter and you make me feel like I can do anything. I'm forever grateful for having you in my life. I look forward to seeing where the journey of life takes us together. Thank you for everything you do. I love you more than everything and I'm forever grateful for everything you've done to help me achieve this goal.

To my Mom, Dad, my Grandpa Jim, and my Ninnie, thank you all for believing in me. Growing up, you made me feel like I could do anything, like I could conquer the world. You helped me to be unafraid in trying new things. You showed me what hard work and dedication looks like. You helped me to understand that anything worth having is worth working hard to have.

More importantly, your love, support, and sacrifices have meant more to me than you could ever know. I love all of you and thank you so much for molding me into the man I am today. It's a debt that could never be repaid. How can I ever thank you enough?

To my good friend, brother, and most valued mentor, Dharshaka "DC" Dias, you opened my eyes to so many things: servant leadership, investing in the betterment of others, personal development, just to name a few.

I've always been driven, but Daily New Year's and this very book would not exist if it had not been for your gift of Darren Hardy's *The Compound Effect* and your gift of guidance. I have valued our friendship and your mentorship these past seven years, and I look forward to being lifelong friends, even if we end up a world apart. Good luck in everything you do, my friend. Godspeed.

To my Element 74 work family, you guys and gals have pushed me, challenged me, supported me, encouraged me, and cheered me on. You are all so important to me, and I appreciate your friendships. To Katie Young specifically, you showed a

Acknowledgments

huge interest in my blog long before you knew its name. When I got hung up and delayed taking it live for the world to see, you challenged me to "just go home and take it live." Daily New Year's was launched the very next morning. Thank you for the challenge and your infectious energy and attitude.

To the men in my Mastermind group, I appreciate our weekly meetings and your willingness to allow me to consume large amounts of our time together discussing my book. The accountability, wisdom, and support you've given me has meant to me. Thanks, bros!

To Carrie Walker, your creative and carefully honed knowledge and expertise with the English language helped to make this book far better than it ever could have been on its own. Your skill in writing and editing is far beyond my comprehension. Rhetorical strategy—what's that? Conceptual planning? Diction? Huh?! I wanted to write a book and share my message, but you helped me take it to a whole new level, and I thank you for that.

I also want to thank Chandler Bolt and the Self Publishing School team. I struggled to make meaningful progress on my book for months. Your course, support, and coaching helped me overcome countless first-time author pitfalls and make my dream a reality. Thanks so much!

Last, but certainly not least, I want to thank you, the reader, for taking the time to read these pages. A message is not a message without people like you to hear it. I hope you gained tremendous value from reading this book, and I hope you use what you've learned here to go out and crush your goals.

Remember, you've got this!

Thank you all!

Austin

Special Thanks

I want to extend a special thank you to the amazing people below for supporting me throughout the process of writing my first book. They've encouraged me, offered me incredible advice, helped me to improve the book and it's resources, and so much more. I honestly could not have done it without this list of amazing Goal Getters. Thank you all!

In no particular order:

Callie Bollinger	Stephen Schott	Jakob Pallesen
Carrie Walker	Audrey Darbonne	Nathan Gautier
Jared Chandler	Greg Pursley	Dharshaka Dias
Erin Miller	Darren Burgfeld	Phillis Bollinger
Chris Behnken	Toni Keesee	Julian Watkins
Rod Jetton	James Faught	Amanda Huber
Daniel Boren	Mike Warren II	Katie Young
Kristen Gautier	Manish Shrestha	Elyse Lyons
Trey Halter	Sarah Monteiro	Isaac Banks
Seamus Layman	Jared McCormick	Tyler Cuba
Trish Erzfeld	Kayla Fitzgerald Ray	Kim Dangerfield
Bob Swayze	Carmela Bortolini	Patrick Dixson
Johnathan Wright	Sam McGinty	John Reith
Valeri A. Vallade	Crystal Banks	Jackie Safont
Chad Fryman	Frank Del Medico	Dane Williams
Deana Luetkenhaus	Jeff Hay	Heather Riggio Foley
Shawn Balint	Justin Pruitt	Kevin Holliday
Dan C Gillogly	Amanda Ellis Flinn	Beth Wingerter
Mark Rigdon	Derek Holland	Chris Levy
Kristin Yates	Isioma Masi	Sarah Wiles
Terri Penrod	Kayla Mason	Beverly Welker
Blake Templeton	Taylor Laws	Tiffany Brosey
Chad Fryman	John McGowan	Megan Frank
Christy Mershon	Laura Fumis	Tina Schlosser
Scott Allan	Matt Kinder	Jason Wray
Amanda Flinn	Travis Grither	Casey McCraw
Jim Riley	Shelley Kaiser	Jeff Mott
Matt Phillips	Chris Molina	Varonnica Kirn
Justin Dambach	Jennifer Teske	Carmela Bortolini
Jennifer Osburn	Toby Long	Hollie Shipley
John Link	Jessica Harrison	Lavonne Ayoub
Mike Poglese	Mark Rigdon	April Smith
Justine Lyn Victoria Edmondson	Kimmberly Wotipka	Stephanie Ridgeway German

Endnotes

1   Tony Robbins and James Altucher, "In pursuit of your why | Tony and James Altucher on the importance of purpose and the tyranny of 'how'," December 21, 2017, in The Tony Robbins Podcast, produced by Robbins Research International, podcast, MP3 audio, 0:32:25, accessed April 14, 2018, https://tonyrobbins.libsyn.com/in-pursuit-of-your-why-tony-and-james-altucher-on-the-importance-of-purpose-and-the-tyranny-of-how.

2   Simon Sinek, "Start with Why", Simon Sinek INC, accessed April 14, 2018, www.startwithwhy.com.

3   Simon Sinek, "Start with Why", Simon Sinek INC, accessed April 14, 2018, www.startwithwhy.com.

4   "Projection," Urban Dictionary, accessed December 13, 2019, https://www.urbandictionary.com/define.php?term=Projection.

5   Tom Bradbury, Meteorology and Flight: Pilot's Guide to Weather. (A & C Black Publishers Ltd, third edition, 2004)

6   Brian Tracy, Goals!: How to Get Everything You Want — Faster Than You Ever Thought Possible (Berrett-Koehler Publishers; Second edition, 2010), 154.

7   Medical Dictionary for the Health Professions and Nursing. S.v. "congenital amputation." Accessed December 30, 2019. https://medical-dictionary.thefreedictionary.com/congenital+amputation

8   Bethany Pico, "Kyle Maynard gives 'No Excuses' speech," Liberty University, Liberty University News Service, October 21, 2011, http://www.liberty.edu/news/index.cfm?PID=18495&MID=39880.

9   "Kyle Maynard, Quadruple Amputee, Reaches Mt. Kilimanjaro Peak," Huffpost, January 17, 2012, https://www.huffpost.com/entry/kyle-maynard-quadruple-am_n_1209654.

10   Kirsti Buick, "From Being 'Lucky to Be Alive' to Winning One of the UK's Toughest Fitness Competitions," Women's Health, March 12, 2019, https://www.womenshealthmag.com/uk/fitness/a29664072/turf-games-fittest-in-the-city-winner/.

11   Dr. Gail Matthews, "Study Focuses On Strategies for Achieving Goals, Resolutions," Dominican University of California, April 18, 2019, https://www.dominican.edu/dominicannews/study-highlights-strategies-for-achieving-goals.

12   Thomas Smale, "9 Quotes From the 'Shark Tank' Stars to Inspire You to Reach Your Goals," Entrepreneur, February 11, 2015, https://www.entrepreneur.com/article/242746.

13   Michael Hyatt, "When and How to Use Habits to Achieve Your Goals," Michael Hyatt (blog), January 23, 2017, www.michaelhyatt.com/habits-achieve-goals.

14   Nick Bunkley, "Joseph Juran, 103, Pioneer in Quality Control, Dies," The New work Times, March 3, 2008, https://www.nytimes.com/2008/03/03/business/03juran.html.

15   Oxford University Press, "Human Development Report 1992," United Nations Development Program (1992), June 8, 2019, http://hdr.undp.org/sites/default/files/reports/221/hdr_1992_en_complete_nostats.pdf.

16   Paula Rooney, "Microsoft's CEO: 80-20 Rule Applies To Bugs, Not Just Features," The Channel Company, June 8 , 2019, https://www.crn.com/news/security/18821726/microsofts-ceo-80-20-rule-applies-to-bugs-not-just-features.htm.

17   Mark Murphy, "Neuroscience Explains Why You Need To Write Down Your Goals If You Actually Want To Achieve Them," Forbes, April 15, 2018, https://www.forbes.com/sites/markmurphy/2018/04/15/neuroscience-explains-why-you-need-to-write-down-your-goals-if-you-actually-want-to-achieve-them/#3e4ab9d97905.

18   Kendra Cherry, "Hippocampus Role in the Limbic System," Verywell Mind, About, Inc. (Dotdash), October 23, 2019, https://www.verywellmind.com/what-is-the-hippocampus-2795231.

19   Grant Cardone, "Write Your Goals Down, First Thing Each Day," Grant Cardone, Grant Cardone Training Technologies, December 13, 2019, https://grantcardone.com/write-your-goals-down-first-thing-each-day/.

20   Brian Tracy, "The Golden Hour (Continued)," Brian Tracy International, December 13, 2019, https://www.briantracy.com/blog/general/the-golden-

Endnotes

hour-2/.

21   Brian Tracy, Goals!: How to Get Everything You Want — Faster Than You Ever Thought Possible (Berrett-Koehler Publishers; Second edition, 2010), 160-163.

22   Douglas Vermeeren, "Why People Fail to Achieve Their Goals," Reliable Plant, Noria Corporation, December 13, 2019, https://www.reliableplant.com/Read/8259/fail-achieve-goals.

23   Haley Zaremba, "How Much Fuel Does It Take To Get To The Moon?," HuffPost, August 8, 2017, https://www.huffpost.com/entry/how-much-fuel-does-it-take-to-get-to-the-moon_b_598a35b5e4b030f0e267c83d.

24   "How to Stay Motivated" SEMrush, accessed August 2, 2018, https://www.semrush.com/info/how%20to%20stay%20motivated

25   "Define: Motivation," Google Dictionary, accessed August 2, 2018, https://www.google.com/search?q=google+dictionary&oq=google+dic&aqs=chrome.0.0j69i57j0l4.1720j0j4&sourceid=chrome&ie=UTF-8#dobs=motivation.

26   TeachThought Staff, "The Definition Of Intrinsic Motivation," TeachThought, August 28, 2017, https://www.teachthought.com/learning/the-definition-of-intrinsic-motivation/

27   Tim Ferris and Michael Gervais "How to Overcome Anxiety and Stress – with Adviser to Olympians, Michael Gervais (#256)," August 2, 2018, in The Tim Ferris Show, produced by Tim Ferris, podcast, MP3 audio, 1:00:27, accessed October 31, 2017, https://tim.blog/2017/08/02/michael-gervais.

28   "Edison Files The Practical Incandescent Light Bulb," Edison Museum, December 13, 2019, https://edisonmuseum.americommerce.com/content3399.html?pageCatID=2&pageID=4.

29   Jennifer Latson, "How Edison Invented the Light Bulb — And Lots of Myths About Himself," Time, Time USA LLC, October 21, 2014, https://time.com/3517011/thomas-edison/.

About the Author

Austin Bollinger is the founder of Daily New Year's, a blog and podcast dedicated to helping people ditch their old, tired resolutions, and instead, achieve massive success in their lives every day through the power of daily goal setting.

Austin is on a mission to build a community of Goal Getters—a group of people who are focused on becoming Better Every day and living life to the fullest. His aim is to help inspire people around the world to take massive action towards their dreams every day, not just for a few weeks at the beginning of each year.

Austin lives in Missouri with his best friend and high school sweetheart, Callie, and their two dogs, Rosie and Lily. He is an aspiring entrepreneur, speaker, coach, and is looking forward to authoring several more books in the future.

Meet him at www.austinbollinger.com.

Goal Getters, Stay in Touch!

AUSTINBOLLINGER.COM

✉ austin@dailynewyears.com
◉ @austinjbollinger
𝕏 @austinbollinger
in linkedin.com/in/austinjbollinger
f facebook.com/austinjbollinger

Next Steps

- **Visit** www.crushyourgoalsbook.com for additional copies of the worksheets and for additional resources.
- **Engage** and get plugged into the Daily New Year's community at www.dailynewyears.com.
- **Connect** with Austin at www.austinbollinger.com or on social media.
- **Leave a review** on Amazon or Goodreads to let others know what you thought of the book.

Work With Austin

Coaching, Workshops, and More.

Austin has a deep seated passion for helping people break free of the things that are holding them back so that they can tap into their true potential and step into their dream lives. We all suffer from things like fear, self-limiting beliefs, doubt, lack of clarity, focus, confidence, or direction—but we don't have to face these things alone.

Austin is available for one-on-one coaching sessions and hands-on workshops and trainings. Through coaching, Austin can help you discover a clear path forward and can help you overcome the obstacles that are standing in your way.

Customized, in-person trainings and workshops are a great way to help teams and groups put the strategies from this book into everyday practice. Get in touch and talk to Austin about booking a training today.

www.austinbollinger.com/work-with-me.

→ reaching your fullest potential

→ When I realized I wasn't ~~content~~ neglecting with my myself life

Enjoy This Book?

Consider sharing it with others!

- ⊘ Share or mention the book on your social media platforms. Use the hashtag **#CrushYourGoals**.

- ⊘ Write a book review on your blog or on a retailer site.

- ⊘ Pick up a copy for friends, family, coworkers, or anyone who you think would enjoy and be challenged by its message.

- ⊘ Share this message on Twitter, Facebook, or Instagram: **I loved #CrushYourGoals by @AustinJBollinger. Get your copy at www.crushyourgoalsbook.com.**

- ⊘ Recommend this book for your workplace, book club, class, or friend group.

Made in the USA
Columbia, SC
03 December 2020